To: Linda & Howard
God bless you
      Huff Harris
      Nov. 29/92

LIVINGWISE
LIVINGWELL

LIVINGWISE
LIVINGWELL

By T. Huffman Harris

Founded 1910
THE CHRISTOPHER PUBLISHING HOUSE
HANOVER, MASSACHUSETTS 02339

COPYRIGHT © 1992
BY T. HUFFMAN HARRIS

Library of Congress Catalog Number 91-73586

ISBN: 0-8158-0450-4

Unauthorized reproduction in any manner is prohibited.

PRINTED IN THE UNITED STATES OF AMERICA

To eight very special grandchildren
and their dedicated parents, but
above all, to my wife Shirley who
daily brings sunshine into the
lives of others.

Contents

Preface

Chapter I   Perceptions on Life 1

Chapter II   Perceptions on Character 13

Chapter III   Perceptions on Success 27

Chapter IV   Perceptions on Marriage 41

Chapter V   Perceptions on Family 53

Chapter VI   Perceptions on Physical Health 65

Chapter VII   Perceptions on Mental Health 77

Chapter VIII   Perceptions on Spiritual Health 89

Preface

After three score years and ten, the author has learned many valuable lessons in Livingwise Livingwell. This book embraces the philosophy that the only treasures which are truly ours are those we lay up in the hearts of others. Some readers may find this book to be a milestone or watershed in their personal lives, a turning point where their future becomes more meaningful and fulfilling. Other readers may be longing to escape from their prisons of mediocrity, drudgery and boredom. A few readers may even be losing their last shred of hope in a brighter tomorrow that once held much promise. Nowhere in this book, however, will the reader find any quick fixes, fast answers, easy solutions or free lunches in one's pilgrimage through life's uncharted waters. Whatever is achieved in this life has a price!

Countless individuals, young and old alike, may be smiling on the outside but crying on the inside — crying for a new beginning! They may be living lives of quiet desperation, all their hopes and dreams fading into the twilight. But God gave us options and choices in life. He gave us intellect and vision to map our own way and choose how we write our personal Book of Life. Within the pages of this book, many life-changing options are revealed to the reader. Just one improvement in one small area of our personal lives invariably results in improvements in other areas simply because they are interlocking in purpose and action.

Any quality book written to inspire, motivate or teach requires recognition by the reader that one or more areas of one's life could stand a little improvement — attitude, self-esteem, goals, finances, self-discipline, habits, patience, health, peace of mind, career, marriage, family. It could be more than mere chance that you are reading this book — God moves in mysterious ways, His wonders to perform!

T. Huffman Harris
Author

Chapter I
Perceptions on Life

In the bulb is a flower
In the seed an apple tree
In the cocoon hidden promise
Butterflies will soon be free

Life at its best is much like a beautiful flower that has all too brief a lifespan to bloom. However it gives seed to keep the cycle of beauty and goodness alive, its decomposition enriching the soil for its offspring. The flower had a noble purpose and in a real sense it never dies as something of itself is carried on. It is a priceless insight to perceive life as a process of self-discovery with every new experience or situation being a lesson in itself. Life is a pilgrimage through unchartered waters, a complex journey of ebbs and flows. But the dawn of each new day is the first day of the rest of our lives. Today well lived makes a happy memory of yesterday and a vision of hope for tomorrow.

Happy individuals gain a greater understanding of the life process as time goes on, discovering new opportunities for growth and fulfillment. They have a simple faith in God, and believe that people are far more important than things, and that giving is far more rewarding than getting. They savor the simple things in life and see hidden meaning and significance even in common things. They get real meaning *out of life* by finding real meaning *in life*. They find their own tune to whistle in a world rife with discord and confusion. Choosing positive thoughts is fundamental to their general well-being and they make sure that no sediments are allowed to accumulate and clutter up their lives. They know down deep in their hearts that positive thoughts and attitudes rather than circumstances determine personal happiness and peace of mind. Their lives reveal a simple truth to all who really know them — an abundance of goodness is far more important than an abundance of goods.

It is not uncommon for trivial things to crowd out the important. Perspective gives a sense of order and balance to our lives. All of us have two selves, an outer self and an inner self. Our outer self is task-oriented and focuses on getting things done (self-confidence). Our inner self is more reflective and thoughtful, focusing on meaning and values, and finding purpose and significance in our lives. Most of us do not take sufficient time to reflect and gain a perspective on our lives as we are preoccupied with the secular outer self. It is a good habit to set aside a few minutes, preferably at the beginning of each day, to get into a reflective state of mind. Quieting of the mind is essential and is best achieved in solitude. There is no single best way or best time for reflection. Soft music, meditation, devotional reading or a leisurely stroll in a park are some practical ways to wake up the inner self. At certain times it is important to take longer periods of time for reflection, particularly when faced with a major problem or decision. This time of reflection and solitude is an important tuning-in process to put things into perspective. As we achieve a feeling of serenity and listen for guidance from within, we gain a sense of inner peace and balance. As purpose and order become increasingly clear, so does our thinking, our priorities and the answers to life's problems.

Everyday is full of God's miracles if only we could see them. Nature is truly God's physician and magic tranquilizer for the troubled soul. Time can be suspended when we are caught up in the wonders of nature. I strolled for miles one day and became lost in my thoughts and solitude. Stretching out alongside a babbling brook with my head propped on a hollow log, I gazed up at fleecy clouds slowly drifting by. Within moments I became nature's captive audience, specks of Canada geese cutting a perfect 'v' high above. The peaceful silence was gently broken by the mournful call of a mother loon that seemed haunting to the ear. Suddenly a hummingbird zoomed by, darting here and there, drawing nectar from morning glories. The sun's rays glistened from morning dew on a spider's web, shimmering through the needles of a pine sapling. As I gazed in awe, marvelling at the beauty and wonder all around me, my thoughts turned to the Creator of all life and the Author of every good and perfect gift.

Time stood still as I slipped into a peaceful slumber, to be suddenly awakened by distant rumbling. Barely a breeze stirred a leaf as I gazed around. Slowly getting to my feet, I could see thunderheads building rapidly on the western horizon. Within minutes the sky turned black as lightning danced closer and closer accompanied by rumbling thunderclaps. The wind picked up from nowhere and began howling through the trees as I sought shelter in an abandoned cabin. Safely inside, the booming claps of thunder and sheets of driving rain gradually subsided. Soon the sun's rays broke through the thick clouds, forming a brilliant rainbow arched across the sky. As I strolled through the countryside on my homeward journey, I reflected on the awesome power yet boundless love of God, the Maker of all things and Giver of all blessings.

Our lives can be compared with the hourglass and its thousands of grains of sand. The hourglass is made so that only one grain at a time can pass slowly and evenly through the narrow neck of its middle. The functioning of the hourglass is impaired when more than one grain tries to pass through at the same time. With God's help we should pace each day like grains of sand — passing slowly and orderly through an hourglass. With quiet confidence and optimism, we should take one day at a time, knowing that the tasks ahead of us are never greater than the Power within us. The following prayer has helped many individuals gain perspective in the hustle and bustle of daily living:

> [1]Slow me down, Lord! Ease the pounding of my heart by the quieting of my mind. Steady my harried pace with a vision of the eternal reach of time. Give me, amidst the confusions of my day, the calmness of the everlasting hills. Break the tensions of my nerves with the soothing music of singing streams that live in my memory. Help me to know the magic restoring power of sleep. Teach me the art of taking minute vacations, of slowing down to appreciate the beauty and wonder of nature, to chat with a friend (especially one in need), to read a few passages of Scripture. Remind me each day that there is more to life than increasing its pace, that precious moments of solitude can help untangle the threads of hectic living. Remind me that the best things in life are like the towering oak that grows great and strong because it grows slowly and well. Slow me down, Lord, and give me the insight to send my roots deep into the soil of life's enduring values, so that I may grow in Thy wisdom.

---

[1]W. A. Peterson (Prayer abbreviated and revised from original.)

Our secular society rushes on in its quest for the fountain of happiness. The more knowledge we acquire, the less wisdom we seem to have. The more financial security we gain, the more discontented we seem to become. The more pleasures we experience, the less meaning and purpose we seem to find in life. Like a restless sea, nothing permanent or fulfilling seems to come from tangible material things. The fountain of true happiness which makes life really satisfying and worthwhile often remains illusive, leaving countless individuals disillusioned with life, yet still searching. Superficial happiness which depends on pleasant circumstances is very fleeting. When circumstances change (as they inevitably do), this kind of happiness evaporates like early morning fog in the heat of the sun. The contentment which brings enduring worth to life is less dependent on continuing favorable circumstances and survives even when things are not going our way. It needs no outward stimulus but dwells deep within us, giving inner peace and contentment. Genuine happiness cannot be hidden — when we are truly happy we know it, and our face will really show it.

Genuine happiness is an elusive treasure pursued by countless individuals, young and old alike. It is a state of mental well-being and contentment that cannot be hidden but radiates and permeates the lives of others. Happy living is the by-product of caring, sharing and giving. Conversely, the more that our thoughts are directed toward self-gain and selfish interests, the more discontentment is experienced. Selfish pursuits can make us prisoners of adverse circumstances and events which seem to control our lives. There is little time for self-centeredness when we experience the rich rewards of serving others with no thought of self-gain. It is impossible to bring sunshine into the lives of others without any shining on ourselves.

There are lessons to be learned in the fascinating wonders in nature. The commonplace becomes wondrous and the wondrous becomes commonplace when we pause to listen for the voice of God in nature — the whispering of tall trees, the music of a babbling brook, the song of a warbler serenading its mate. The peaceful solitude of the wilderness (with its unspoiled forest, wildlife, streams and lakes) captivates the imagination and brings tranquility to the soul. God is present in different ways, and He can never be reduced to our own limited image of Him.

Each one of us looks at life through different eyes. No two individuals are treading the exact same path in their journey through life. Three men can look at the same tree, yet each can perceive something different that impresses them. One visualizes cordwood for keeping his family warm when winter arrives. Another visualizes board-feet of lumber for building a house. A third sees a masterpiece of God's creation having a value far beyond any firewood or lumber. Two men viewed the tree superficially for their own self-interest, but the third gazed in awe at its grandeur and beauty.

The vast expanse of space beyond the countless stars and galaxies gives us but a glimpse of the wonder and awe of creation. Space is limitless. Our galaxy, the Milky Way, is merely one of countless billions of stars, but it is only a tiny speck in the infinite reaches of space. On the outskirts of this speck glows a yellow dwarf star which is our sun. One of the smallest planets revolving around the sun is the earth upon which we live. Its 23 degree tilt gives us the four seasons of the year. Enormous ocean tides would submerge all six continents twice every day if the moon were much closer to our planet. The earth is the wonder of the universe, a slowly-rotating unique sphere with an infinity of its own, encompassing everything from the busy world of the atom to the limitless mind and spirit of several billion human beings. The movement of the planets through space governs our measurement of time, with every tiny event and moment being a miracle of God's creation.

Each day the sun rises and then sets, the daily cycle repeating itself as the earth continues its steady and orderly rotation. The more things in our lives seem to change, the more they remain the same. Life is much like the streams and rivers that eventually flow into the oceans, yet the oceans are never full. Our lives are much like nature with its seasons, growing and resting imperceptively in stages. But at every stage in life we grow through the process of change and challenge. Life goes on, having its ups and downs, its laughter and tears. Our season here on earth is only a moment in eternity — generations come and generations go. By pursuing ideals that have enduring worth, the goodness and truth in our lives will continue long after we are gone. The only treasures which are truly ours are those we lay up in the hearts of others.

Life is chiefly made up of little things and seemingly insignificant events that have little or no consequence. We tend to live unexamined lives, failing to perceive nature's miracles even in mundane things — a spider web trembling with dewdrops, the eerie hoot of an owl as darkness descends on a wintry wonderland, buds bursting in early spring. God's miracles are all around us, but goodness and beauty are only in the eye of the beholder. We can alter the landscape and contour of a day by the mood of the moment as we savor one of the great wonders of life — the wonder of life itself. The most cherished things in our lives can be of the common variety. All of us can sharpen our awareness and capture the joys that flow from ordinary things. A sense of transcendent meaning lingers beneath the surface of our daily lives when we sense the presence of God in the mundane.

Hummingbirds are a fascinating miracle of nature. Their size, color and even the shape of their beaks vary depending on their habitat and source of nectar. Their maneuverability during feeding and flight is not only spectacular but incredible from a scientific standpoint. The hummingbird is the smallest creature in the animal world, yet migrates up to 2,000 miles twice a year. During flight, the high-speed vibration of its wings requires considerable energy, necessitating frequent nourishment of nectar. Its rate of heartbeat increases during flight up to three times its normal 400 beats per minute. At night the hummingbird is the ultimate efficiency expert as it settles into a comatose state to minimize consumption of energy. Its heartbeat drops from a daytime normal rate of 400 to only 30 beats per minute, and its body temperature drops from a daytime normal of 110°F to 55°F. The tiny hummingbird is but one of God's miraculous wonders in nature which we tend to take for granted.

Discernment is the ability to perceive the good from the bad, the genuine from the counterfeit, the natural from the artificial. Discerning individuals are sensitive to subtle clues and see much more than the obvious. They live by the basic truth that every individual has to live with himself, so they see to it that they always have good company. They realize that the best reformers are those who begin on themselves. They have a positive outlook on life and believe that the dawn of each new day is a fresh beginning in life's pilgrimage. They know that those things which preoccupy or dazzle the secular world are seldom in the mainstream of God's work.

To the discerning, prominence is not the same as eminence nor is the celebrity of the hour apt to be the sage of the ages. The discerning individual does not yearn for ego gratification but channels his thoughts, words and deeds into helping and serving others. For the discerning, success and happiness in life have much to do with an abundance of goodness but little to do with an abundance of goods. Life is perceived as a process of self-discovery, gaining wisdom and understanding and becoming more perceptive to:

> What is important and what is insignificant
> What is absolute and what is relative
> What is needed and what is wanted
> What is right and what is wrong
> What is false and what is true
> What is trivial and what is meaningful
> What is transitory and what is lasting
> What can be changed and what cannot be changed
> What bears good fruit and what bears bad fruit

Today well lived makes a happy memory of yesterday and a vision of hope for tomorrow. Life consists of time and how time is used. Few of us fully grasp the concept that time is a precious gift. There is no past or future time, only the present which we measure in small momentary slices. Our past is recorded and catalogued in various time frames of our memory. Our future is not only uncertain but completely blank as it is not within the focus of our experiences. We can plan, anticipate and shape our future to some extent but we cannot dictate it.

Each one of us is given a daily bank account called TIME. At the beginning of each day a brand new account is opened. No balances or overdrafts are allowed, and any of the day's deposit which we fail to use is lost. We are free to do as we want with each day's deposit — we can use it, abuse it, invest it wisely, waste it foolishly. The choice is ours!

There are two days which should never cause regret or worry. One is YESTERDAY with its share of mistakes and cares, its aches and pains. Yesterday has passed forever — beyond our control. Nothing or no one can bring back yesterday. We cannot undo a single act we performed; we cannot erase a single word we said; we cannot retrieve a single hour we wasted. Regret will not change anything. Yesterday is gone! The other day which should be kept free from worry or anxiety is TOMORROW with its problems and challenges. Although we should plan for tomorrow, we should not be anxious about it. Habitual anxiety reflects a lack of faith and undermines our health and vitality. The joy of living TODAY can be stolen by regrets and worries of yesterdays and tomorrows.

One day as a happy grandfather clock was ticking away one second at a time, another clock said to him, "Just think! We have to tick 3,600 times every single hour, over 86,000 times every single day, over 600,000 times every week, over 31 million times every year!" The more the grandfather clock thought about these astronomical numbers of ticks, the more he labored in his ticking. His ticking became more and more erratic until he almost had a nervous breakdown. "Listen, my friend," said a wise old clock nearby, "happiness is in the present, not in the future or the past." So the grandfather clock wisely concentrated on enjoying each moment, taking one tick at a time. He didn't think of the next tick until he ticked the last tick. How true to life! The future is *now* when we live to the fullest in the *present*.

TODAY is the one and only day we are living right now. Therefore, we should concentrate on one day, TODAY, and live and enjoy it to the fullest. Anyone can fight the battles of just one day with God's help. It is only when we add the burdens of YESTERDAY and TOMORROW that we cannot live and enjoy TODAY to the fullest. By looking for opportunities to brighten and enrich the lives of others, today's good deeds become tomorrow's happy memories. Today is the first day of the rest of our lives. It is your day and mine to make of it what we will.

We must not allow the cares of yesterday or the worries of tomorrow to rob us of the joy of living today. The saddest thing about not living in the present is to 'exist' for a lifetime and completely miss the joy of living each day. By taking one day at a time and making each moment count, it can have a profound effect upon our lives. We can gain a better perspective on life by turning our thoughts to absorbing the beauty and goodness of nature and all God's creation. Our lives will become more serene, with purpose and order becoming increasingly clear as the mist of uncertainty and confusion evaporates.

Procrastination is the cause of many lost opportunities in our lives. When a friend of mine was a little girl, she was impressed with a beautiful piece of pure silk yardage which her mother kept in the sewing room. The material was made in China and given to her mother years ago by a special friend. Often the little girl's mother talked about what she might make from the beautiful material. But she never got up the courage to cut into it for fear of making a mistake and ruining it. The sad part of the story is that she never did make anything with it. Many years later when she died at age eighty-six, her daughter, now married with a daughter of her own, noticed the material still on the shelf in her mother's sewing room. With great anticipation of finally using it, she gently unfolded the lovely silk yardage only to find it was badly faded. Now it was good for nothing!

TODAY is a fragment of a priceless gift called TIME which cannot be stored or retrieved. Having too much time on our hands may be a warning signal that our lives could be devoid of purpose, direction or worthwhile goals. Time is limited and so very important. Life is now, TODAY! We can resolve today to make our lives more fulfilling and rewarding by using our time rather than misusing it. We should always remember that the roots and the fruits of contented living lie within ourselves more than in our circumstances.

Wisdom is found on the lips of the discerning (Proverbs 10:13). Discernment and insight are intangible qualities that give substance to our lives. These important qualities are vividly illustrated in this story about a brash youth and a wise old man. The youth resented the fact that people of all ages went to the old man for counsel. Finally he came up with a devilish scheme to trap the old man and prove him wrong. He took a young bird from its nest and, hiding it in his hands behind his back, said to the old man, "Since you are so clever, is the object that I have in my hands dead or alive?" If the old man answered "dead", he would show him the live bird. If the old man answered "alive", he would crush it in his hands and show him a dead bird. The wise old man studied the brash youth and looking intently into his eyes, said "The answer is in your hands!"

The mind chooses and decides, but the heart is the fortress of the soul. Discerning intangibles and weighing their relative importance are usually important in making complex decisions. By contrast, routine decisions are repetitive by nature and usually involve only two straightforward options. Repetitive decisions have much in common with a 'chicken sexer' in a hatchery who sorts newborn chicks by sex. Each fuzzy, yellow chick is grasped, instantly identified by gender and placed in either a female or male compartment. This simple task can be performed without error by the chicken sexer at a rate of over a thousand an hour. How simple life would be if all or even most of life's decisions were that straightforward!

However, sooner or later, all of us experience decisions that are more like those of a 'hide grader' who must discern the potential of each hide, taking into account its color, smell, pliability, strength and other less tangible characteristics. The hides are sorted and graded into more than twenty categories. The decision-making process is laden with intangible and complex options which are measured in degrees and shades of differences. Most choices that affect the course of our lives are much like those of the hide grader but have little in common with the chicken sexer.

The giant redwood trees of California tower as much as three hundred feet above the ground. These magnificent trees have an unusually shallow root system which spreads out in all directions to capture the maximum amount of surface moisture. Seldom does a large redwood tree stand alone because the shallow roots would be uprooted during high winds. That is why we find these giant trees clustered in groves with their root systems intertwined, supporting and sustaining one another in stormy weather. Like the redwood trees we need each other especially during the storms of life. Yet, some of us tend to be an island unto ourselves, living barren lonely lives with no close personal relationships.

Feelings and emotions have an impelling influence on human behavior. Reason often seems to be dominated by feelings as countless individuals live and breathe like a fluctuating tide going to and fro from "lows" to "highs." The body, mind and soul are inseparable, with the ills of one invariably affecting the others. When negative emotions are allowed to run deep and out of control, they can be like a rampaging river that overflows its banks. They are not restricted by principles of logic, psychological understanding or scriptural truth which fortify the banks. Negative emotions such as fear, discouragement, anger, guilt or depression often play too dominate a role at crucial times in our pilgrimage through life.

Like the mighty lift of the ocean tide freeing a battered ship from rocky reefs, the spiritual dimension of our lives can make all the difference.

Some years ago, design engineers were investigating supporting structures to carry a new bridge across a portion of New York's harbor. An old barge loaded with a cargo of rocks and bricks lay buried deep in the muddy bottom. It was located where support structures for the bridge were required. All conventional measures for moving the barge failed due to its weighty cargo. Finally one bright engineer conceived a plan of securing the sunken wreck by long chains to several floating barges directly above. The slack chains were tightened as low tide approached. Soon the chains creaked as the floating barges gradually rose higher and higher with the water level. As high tide arrived, the sunken wreck was slowly lifted from its viselike grip and finally freed from its watery grave. So it is with our lives! We can become mired, gripped by disillusionment and despair, and bound by fear and uncertainty. But with God's help and guidance we can rise above any misfortunes that shackle our hopes and dreams.

Growers of hybrid lilies know that removing the spent blossoms of the previous day will increase the plant's blooming capacity. With the weight of yesterday's blossoms removed, the stalks rise up, ready to flower the following day. So it should be in our lives — the cares of yesterday should also be shed, enabling the opportunities of today to be fully realized. Brooding over past events or worrying about the future is a waste of mental energy as well as being detrimental to our physical and spiritual well-being. Bitter residues of the past or apprehensions of the future can surely sabotage the mind and undermine our general well-being.

Like the law of supply and demand in the world of business, there is an invisible spiritual law of Cause and Effect that regulates all human affairs. As we sow, so shall we reap — just as surely as night follows day, *effect* will surely follow *cause*. Disregarding this law is the root cause of most personal and social ills. This spiritual law is the Way of Life that is diametrically opposite to the way of selfish human nature. It is the way of love instead of greed, the way of giving instead of getting, the way of caring instead of neglecting, the way of empathy instead of indifference. It is the way of concern for others instead of self-concern. It is the way of cooperation instead of competition; the way of humility and forgiveness instead of pride and self-righteousness. It is the way of God-centeredness instead of self-centeredness which can be summed up in a personal code to live by: "Do unto others as you would have them do unto you."

There is so much that we cannot fully understand in our lives! Yet we know that without planting there could be no harvest; without birth there could be no life; without injustice there could be no justice; without suffering there could be no compassion; without need there could be no worthwhile service; without problems there could be no solutions; without challenges there could be no successes. The real meaning of events in our lives is revealed by our response to the events rather than the events themselves. Our thoughts and our beliefs are not just part of our lives, they are central to our lives. At times our heart and mind wage a battle — our heart being the fortress of the soul while our mind chooses and decides. Our mind may deceive us but our heart never!

Sooner or later all of us experience at least one watershed or crossroad that significantly affects the course of our lives. At the time it may seem a relatively minor event or chance encounter, but in retrospect it had a great impact on our lives. Sometimes a casual acquaintance or even a total stranger can have a profound effect, while other times a major illness, accident or untimely death of a loved one can leave an indelible imprint.

Most people at one time or another have experienced a yearning for something fundamental that is missing in their lives. This yearning may lay dormant for long days, months or sometimes even years. Then, for no apparent reason, the agitation begins again — maybe even stronger than before. When we are willing to examine the purpose and meaning of our lives, then in a profound sense we have made a start toward nourishing the seeds of greatness that lie within each one of us. Satisfying this divine urge to experience the fullness of life at its best gives an inner peace and contentment that we have never known before. Such an experience awaits any of us who admits that, alone without God, we cannot master life with all of its problems and uncertainties. The foundation for happiness and true success in life lies in an ever-deepening personal faith and trust in God. We all pass through this world but once; if there is any kindness we can show or any good thing we can do, let us do it now, for we shall not pass this way again!

Chapter II
Perceptions on Character

Human nature may have its imperfections but the elusive quality of character sets us apart. The good life is not a game of chance but a matter of choice. Moral and ethical standards guide and direct us in charting our journey through life, enabling us to perceive the true nature of things and to wisely choose the right path. Our day-to-day conduct and decisions reflect our character which is molded and strengthened through self-discipline but undermined by permissiveness. Each week of our lives becomes seven living letters for others to read. The challenge each day is to be an influence for good in our temporal society, yet not ruled by its values.

Character-building is a lifetime process which should begin in the early formative years. Responsible behavior does not come naturally or instinctively but must be learned and practiced. The development of character is a continuing process of perceiving and choosing the good rather than the bad and demonstrating personal integrity at all times. Often this means that we must be willing to stand out from the crowd rather than becoming part of it. At times it means being different and unpopular, being willing to 'stick our neck out' and take a stand for what we know is right. It means that we must resist the temptation to be like the chameleon which changes its color to blend in with its surroundings.

When torn between compromising our moral or ethical standards and our conscience, we should always listen to our conscience. The mind chooses and decides but the heart is the fortress of the soul.

Periodically it is a good idea to spend some quiet time in reflection, taking an honest inventory of our lives. We can move to new levels of growth and fulfillment by carefully examining and assessing our lives. The best reformers are usually those who begin on themselves. We should examine areas of our lives where we could improve, but equally important we should assess our strengths and aptitudes. How we feel towards ourselves and the world around us influences our thoughts, attitudes and beliefs.

By developing a perceptive frame of mind we are better able to see every personal experience as a lesson in itself — a lesson of character in every adverse experience and a lesson of humility in every good fortune. The greatest lessons in life are learned in times of adversity rather than when things are going our way. Every adversity can be a character-builder rather than an obstacle, a challenge rather than a problem. Perseverance during adversity not only strengthens character but ensures success sooner or later. The salmon overcomes many obstacles as it swims upstream mile-after-mile, eventually reaching its spawning goal.

The story is told about a young author who experienced a heart-breaking disappointment that could have permanently embittered a lesser man. He decided to write a serious book. Days stretched into weeks and weeks into months, as he arduously wrote and rewrote page after page. With four long years of tedious work came completion of his lengthy manuscript. After destroying all his earlier notes and drafts, he took the final handwritten draft of his manuscript to his trusted friend for evaluation. Hour after hour his friend poured over it page after page, realizing that he was reading a great literary achievement. All day and late into the night he read on and on. Finally he fell asleep reading in his den and the pile of manuscript pages slipped off his lap among newspapers on the floor. When he awoke he turned out his reading lamp and went to bed.

Early the next morning the maid noticed all the messy papers on the floor. As was her custom in the past, she burned all the papers in the stove. When the author's friend awoke and learned what had happened he went to the young author and told him about the disheartening accident. Overcoming his initial shock and despair, the young author said that he would start over again. Although it was a long, difficult process, he persevered and finally completed his second manuscript. The publication of his book gave the author an even greater sense of achievement than he would have experienced had the accident not occurred. The greatest achievements and blessings in our lives often come out of misfortunes and injustices.

The development of character is a gradual process which can be strengthened or weakened by adversity. Some individuals become better while others become bitter and are left with permanent scars. A farmer planted sugar-maple saplings around the perimeter of a pasture field. A few years later, using the trees as fence posts he strung barbed wire around the field. It was a traumatic experience for the young trees as the wire was stapled deep into the tender bark. More than a half century later the grove of large sugar maples revealed some important lessons of character. Some trees were permanently injured and severely disfigured as they fought against the barbed wire over the years. They became its victim, long anguished scars distorting their trunks.

Other trees however accepted the barbed wire and made the best of it, incorporating the wire into their trunks as they grew over the years. They became masters rather than victims, the wire disappearing smoothly into the bark on one side and emerging from the other. Internal forces had reacted positively in a healing process rather than negatively as in some other trees. A certain toughness of character is often born in adversity but seldom found in a life of comfort and ease.

> [1]*Good Timber*
> A tree that never had to fight
> For sun and rain and air and light
> Never became a forest king
> But lived and died a scrubby thing.
> Good timber does not grow in ease
> The stronger wind the tougher trees
> As they hold converse with the stars
> Their broken branches show the scars
> Of many strains and storms and strife
> This is the Common Law of Life.

What happens 'to' us is not as important as what happens 'in' us. Such was the experience of Joni Eareckson.[2] At the age of seventeen, she was the victim of a diving accident that left her totally and permanently paralyzed from the neck down. Following the accident, Joni went through agonizing weeks as she struggled to accept and adjust to her shattering handicap which would leave her confined to a wheelchair

---

[1]*Good Timber* is quoted from memory; unable to verify or locate source.
[2]Eareckson, Joni (Zondervan, Grand Rapids, 1976)

for the rest of her life. Her initial bitterness, self-pity, uncertainty and depression gradually dissipated, as she discovered invaluable spiritual truths through daily reading and meditating on God's Word. Joni's terrible tragedy and misfortune had a life-changing silver lining which has had a profound impact on the lives of countless others, young and old alike. She praises and serves the Lord by living a God-centered life of sharing and caring, bringing inspiration and joy to the lives of others. She has become a skillful artist using only her mouth to hold the brush. Two films have been made which reveal the transformation in her life following her accident. Joni is a living witness that God uses all things to work together for the good of those who love Him. What happened 'in' Joni following what happened 'to' Joni demonstrates how God's love is greater than any adversity.

Perseverance produces character, and character — hope. Talent alone never achieves worthwhile goals. Nothing really worthwhile in life can be achieved without commitment and perseverance. Perseverance based on strong commitment is essential. Noah Webster labored diligently for 21 years until finally at the age of seventy, he completed his incomparable American Dictionary. Thomas Edison was stricken with scarlet fever as a child, which left him partially deaf. At the age of twelve, with practically no formal education, he was forced to take a full-time job to help support his poverty-stricken family. Self-discipline and perseverance were vital personal qualities in realizing his goals. Over a forty-year span, he applied for more than one thousand patents relating to his numerous inventions. Edison persevered in his countless experiments, having many failures and disappointments. His humble beginnings and misfortunes were no barrier to his great achievements.

Any ordinary person can become extraordinary by developing strong character. Well-deserving people may often appear to finish last but usually they are running a different race. Individuals with deep moral convictions and integrity are untouched and unspoiled by greed and corruption which poison the lives of so many people. There seems to be a human tendency to rationalize improper or unethical conduct. But beliefs and convictions based on Biblical truths do not succumb to impulsive temptations or ulterior motives. Honesty, justice and kindness form a moral philosophy which constitutes the foundation of ethics. Personal integrity involves a sense of values and standard of conduct by which character is shaped. This unwritten code is the power of conscience which governs our lives. The ultimate test of good character is doing what is right at all times even when no one is looking.

Character is the sum total of what we really are. Reputation however is what others think we are which often is not an accurate portrayal of our character. We should always remember that a good reputation is easier lost than recovered. Character is what we know we are, including our hidden strengths and weaknesses. Honesty and integrity are prime virtues of good character which transcend skills and accomplishments. Knowledge and education alone are no guarantee of good character. Self-discipline and perseverance mold and strengthen character but permissiveness and instant gratification weaken it. The day-to-day problems and circumstances of life provide challenges and opportunities to strengthen and test our character. Our ethics and moral standards set us apart, influencing our decisions and personal conduct.

Truth seldom emerges from conflicting opinions. Strong conflicting opinions usually generate more heat than light. Paradoxically individuals with strong opinions often have weak convictions. Opinions tell us little about an individual but convictions tell us much. Opinions can sway like grass in the wind and vary widely even within the same school of thought. Experts in the same specialized field often have conflicting opinions; even when they agree they may well be mistaken. Logic, reason and science are necessary in solving complex problems but do not hold the key for understanding their root cause. The greatest good stems from deep convictions and commitments rather than from strong opinions.

The development of strong character is a gradual process, much like the molding of clay by the potter. He kneads it, works it, tears it apart and presses it together. He wets it, then dries it and lets it lie for awhile without touching it. When it is very pliable, the potter resumes his work of making a unique vessel of the clay. He forms it into shape, then trims and polishes it. He dries it in the sun, then bakes it in the oven and finally it becomes a finished vessel fit for use. God is the Master Potter and we are the clay to be molded and fashioned in His image. Sometimes we rely only on our own knowledge and strength, trying to do the work of the Potter rather than seeking guidance from the Master.

Where our treasure is, there our heart will be also. As we think deep down in our hearts, so are we (Proverbs 23:7). The eternal law of life dictates that we become what we think. Our thoughts are the fathers of our attitudes and shape our general outlook on life. Our thoughts, our efforts and our time are captured by those things which are important to us. Our values and priorities in life are revealed by our choices and decisions, by what we do and how we act in our daily lives. Occasionally it is beneficial for all of us to spend some time in quiet solitude, meditating and reflecting on our pilgrimage through life's uncharted waters.

It is much easier to identify individuals with integrity than it is to pinpoint what makes them so. Like so many other virtues, integrity is more easily recognized than defined. It is what we are, more than what we are not; what we do, more than what we do not do. Individuals with integrity strive to live by their convictions and seek out friends who share their moral and ethical standards. They know that living a life beyond reproach is more than just a creed, it is a deep personal commitment. Whenever ethics and integrity are at stake, they are willing to stand out from the crowd rather than become lost in it.

Our lives are shaped by our choices and decisions, by how we live and what is important to us. We become what we cherish and value most, those things which occupy our thoughts and time. Many of us crave the temporal things of this world, setting a value on them as if they bestow a special dignity on us. A confusing array of values and role models are presented to our younger generation. The promotion of situational ethics and permissiveness blurs ethical and moral guidelines. Even where Scriptural truths are at stake, any absolute right or wrong falls into a controversial gray area. Attempts are made through man-made laws to achieve some measure of social order and justice but personal ethics and integrity can never be legislated.

Man-made laws are somewhat like animal cages — they can restrain behavior but they cannot alter character. Molding good character and responsible behavior cannot be accomplished by passing more laws or building more prisons. Vice and crime may feed on ignorance and poverty but do not automatically flow from them. Moral choices and responsible behavior are prompted by the conscience which should be kindled early in life. A sense of values needs to be caught in the home before being taught in the school. This unwritten code influences behavior and shapes character — the inner voice of conscience. The ultimate test of ethics and integrity is doing what is right at all times even when no one is looking.

A 12-year-old boy and his father were fishing late one evening from the dock by their secluded family cabin. Bass season would be opening at midnight, just hours away. After catching a few perch and sunfish using worms as bait, the boy decided to practice casting using a silver lure. The reflection of the setting sun made crimson ripples when the lure struck the water with each cast. As darkness descended, the full moon over the lake gave a silvery tinge to the ripples. Suddenly the fishing pole bent wildly as the boy skillfully worked a huge fish alongside the dock. His father watched with a broad smile as the boy cleverly slipped a net over its large head and raised the fish to the dock. It was the largest fish the boy had ever seen in the lake but it was a 'bass.'

Briefly examining the huge fish, the father turned on a flashlight to check his watch. It was 10:30 P.M., ninety minutes before bass season opened. He looked at the large bass, then at his son. "You'll have to put it back, son" he said. "But, Dad!" cried the boy as he looked around the lake. There was no one around, they were all alone. He looked at his father again! His father's eyes and gestures made it clear that his decision was not only final but it was right. The boy slowly worked the lure free from its mouth and lowered the huge bass into the water.

That incident happened 35 years ago. His father has passed on but the memory of this lesson in character development remains as clear to him as the water in the spring-fed lake. The son, now with a 12-year-old boy of his own, spends weekends and vacations with his family at the same cabin where they fish off the same dock. His father taught him that ethics and integrity are simply matters of doing what is right, especially when no one is looking. These virtues need to be learned early in life as they shape conduct and behavior which are the essence of character.

Our secular society favors a permissive value-free philosophy that gives more weight to opinions than to moral convictions. This philosophy breeds situational ethics and a growing gray area between what is right and what is wrong. Our permissive culture accepts and promotes the concept that individuals have the right and authority to set their own moral and ethical standards. Personal freedom and civil rights are stressed while personal responsibility and accountability are too often disregarded. Legal loopholes and interpretations of man-made laws have contributed to a growing indifference and cynicism to rules and standards of behavior. But individuals with strong character and deep moral convictions are unspoiled by their secular environment.

Hypocrisy is pretending outwardly what we are not inwardly. When it becomes ingrained in one's character, hypocrisy takes on a mask of deception and self-righteousness until much of life becomes a charade. In its early stages, hypocrisy is not clearly evident, making it difficult to discern and deal with effectively. There is an inherent self-destructiveness in hypocrisy as it undermines personal credibility and integrity when it is exposed. Honesty, sincerity and humility are virtues that do not submit to hypocrisy in any form.

Prejudice is a common problem because it has its roots in pride and self-righteousness. The word 'prejudice' means making a judgment without full knowledge of all the facts. The stronger the prejudice, the further the distance between opinion and truth. Extreme prejudice can rob its victim of a fair trial in the court of reason. Education can do much to reduce or neutralize prejudice by improving tolerance and understanding. However, education cannot eliminate prejudice because in the final analysis it is a spiritual problem — we should never judge others until we have walked in their shoes.

Envy is inherent in our very nature but can be overcome with a spirit of gratitude. It is impossible to have peace of mind and contentment when we harbor envy in our hearts. Envy can shrink our circle of friends, undermine our health, distort our values and alienate us from God. Paradoxically, envy makes others' blessings our curses, others' fortunes our misfortunes, others' successes our failures. Prolonged envy can literally shrivel and wither away the soul. Greed, closely allied with envy, fosters inner discontent and permeates most areas of our secular society.

Pride can take many forms — spiritual, intellectual, social or material. The sin of pride consists essentially of undue self-regard. By definition pride is an inordinate sense of our own importance and is closely associated with vanity. Self-righteousness is evidence of spiritual pride which leaves little room for a spirit of gratitude. Spiritual pride trusts in our own virtues rather than the grace of God. Intellectual pride manifests itself in arrogance, forgetting that our knowledge is largely the product of the labors of others who have gone before us. Social pride primarily manifests itself in economic discrimination, while material pride is an obsession with things we have or want. The sin of pride fails to recognize that all that we have including life itself are gifts from God.

Do not try to win the approval of man; rather, be the servant of Christ (Galatians 1:10). Although it is good to have self-esteem, we should guard against excessive or false pride. When things are going our way, there is a tendency to forget God and trust in our own virtues. In the intellectual area of our lives, we often forget that the talents that we possess are gifts from God. In the material and social areas of our lives, we tend to place undue emphasis on possessions and status. Some of us have an undue self-regard and an inordinate sense of our own importance. Excessive pride is a sin and is closely associated with vanity (eagerness for admiration). Invariably pride is devoid of a spirit of gratitude or humility.

Stripped of human rationalization for irresponsible behavior, the bottom line is that bad habits are a personal choice. Any bad habit can lead to addictive behavior, which is essentially a moral rather than a medical problem. Every mature individual has the power of will but some do not exercise it. Thought is the author of every good or bad act. Thoughts play a dominate role in most temptations leading to irresponsible behavior. Most bad habits and addictions are primarily self-induced and perpetuated. Once an addictive pattern is established, it is very difficult to break the habit as the individual becomes a slave to the destructive behavior. In essence, bad habits and destructive behavior are synonymous. Self-control and personal responsibility are virtues of good character which are demonstrated by abstinence in all bad things and moderation in others.

Many individuals succeed in overcoming harmful, debilitating habits and lifestyles. Without exception, their success against temptation is neither instant nor automatic but takes self-discipline, effort and time. Harmful habits often begin as little cobwebs but end up as powerful chains. Tempting situations in life present a mirror to our inner selves that can teach us vital lessons. Temptation provides us with an opportunity to come down solidly on the side of personal responsibility and accountability. The more often we succeed, the greater insight and understanding we gain of our inner selves. We will find that it is easier to suppress the first wrong desire than to satisfy all that follow it.

Temptation deceives us by promising much more than it can deliver. It takes advantage of impulses, moods and whims. Timid souls and shallow thinking usually succumb to temptation or instant gratification. Striving against the shackles of harmful habits increases self-esteem as feelings of triumph and success flow from bold decisions. As we become more aware that our behavior and demeanor reflect our real character, we begin to take charge of our thoughts and feelings. In life as in sports, it is facing challenges and obstacles that make the game worthwhile. Happiness and contentment are found by those who daily seek to do what is right and pleasing to God.

Responsible individuals know they are accountable for their habits and behavior. Our affluent, permissive culture fosters the philosophy that individuals who do harm to themselves or others are *'victims'* of biological or social forces over which they have no control. Repeated offenders are labelled as *'sick'* rather than irresponsible. This false philosophy ignores the fact that countless individuals face personal temptations every day but successfully resist them. For example, cigarette smoking is initially a bad habit not an addiction. The withdrawal symptoms of this or any other bad habit can make the battle against temptation quite difficult. But the battle can be won as evidenced by the millions of ex-smokers who quit on their own without any professional treatment. They simply decided to quit their bad habit and exercised willpower to do so.

By definition, addiction is a state in which the individual cannot help himself. Addiction is basically a moral problem of character rather than a medical problem. Deviant behavior and self-destructive habits are the cause not the result of addiction. The addict — smoking, drugs, alcohol, gambling, extramarital affairs — is the loser in the battle of temptation primarily due to indifference or lack of self-worth. The most effective treatment for any addiction or self-destructive habit is to hold individuals responsible for their own behavior. Ironically, many worthwhile public programs in education, health care and social welfare are financed in large part through regressive taxation on lotteries, alcohol, tobacco and legalized gambling.

Our daily lives reveal our values and priorities. Those things which are important to us capture our thoughts, our efforts and our time. There is more to the good life than just drawing a paycheck or watching television. It is never too late (or too soon) to strive for a worthwhile goal which by its very nature requires effort and perseverance. The strength of character and sense of self-worth that will be gained far exceed any personal sacrifices. Self-worth reflects the value that we place on ourselves. It often fluctuates, rising when things are going well but dropping when things go badly. One ingredient for building and sustaining positive self-esteem is to make and *keep* commitments. However, it is more difficult to keep private commitments than public ones as no one ever knows when we break them — to be more patient and kind, to be less irritable and critical, to be more others-centered and less self-centered. All of us can improve in some small area of our lives by making a private commitment that we know we can keep. As we begin building a track record of private successes, any feeling of mediocrity is replaced by an exhilarated feeling of self-worth.

Individuals who believe in their personal worth seem to be like magnets for opportunities. They demonstrate a love for people through a network of long-lasting relationships. They use their natural aptitudes to advantage and develop skills in those areas where their interests gravitate. Conversely, other individuals have a way of being their own worst enemy as nothing seems to work out for them. Their problems are often of their own making and usually magnified in their minds. Negative thoughts of despair and self-pity can dominate and smother any feelings of self-worth. Low self-esteem can eventually lead to a slipshod lifestyle devoid of self-discipline.

Strong character often manifests itself in the midst of self-doubt and adversity. In 1843 Charles Dickens, a budding young author and 31-year-old father of four, was deeply troubled over his mounting financial debts. By early October he began taking long evening walks to alleviate his depression. Late one evening as he neared home, Dickens experienced a sudden flash of inspiration for a cheerful glowing tale. Within minutes he was at his desk writing feverishly. His manuscript grew page by page, the characters magically taking life as the story unfolded. Working from early morning to late each night he was reluctant to lay aside his manuscript even briefly.

The story, *A Christmas Carol*, held a strange mastery over Dickens. He finished the manuscript on December 2, the book was published by mid-December and the first edition was sold out by Christmas Eve. Its heartwarming message spread far and wide, his little Christmas tale bringing soul-satisfying joy and inspiration to countless millions, young and old alike. Dickens died in 1870 but his universally loved novel illustrates a simple truth — *inspiring thoughts have timeless value when they are given life in print.*

We can build a healthy self-image through visualization whereby we picture ourselves with poise and confidence when facing a difficult challenge or adversity. When such positive images are burned deeply into our minds through daily repetition, they become part of the subconscious. Over a period of time, we will find that the more we envision beneficial things happening in our personal lives, the more likely they will actually occur. We will also find that the more that our thoughts, words and deeds are focused on service and love for others, the greater will be our rewards.

Human nature may be imperfect, but our personality and character set us apart. A graceful dignity flows with ease from a warm personality and feelings of self-worth. All of us have potential goodness in our hearts that all too rarely bursts to the surface. This goodness often lies dormant until it is kindled by a spirit of gratitude. We cannot grow in the ways of God and remain the same. Our daily walk through life is given direction, meaning and purpose when our lives are attuned to God's love.

Conscience is a personal unwritten code which shapes our character. This inner voice of conscience can be scarred and dulled until its whisper is no longer heard. Situational ethics and a confusing array of values and moral guidelines can undermine the conscience which was created by God for our own good. A sensitive conscience guides us in making right decisions and sticking to the high road in our pilgrimage through life. Guilt is to the soul what pain is to the body, a warning signal that something is amiss. It helps us to see that something is wrong and should be changed. Our conscience gives us a message of disapproval whenever we are tempted to compromise our personal integrity.

A spirit of gratitude is a natural by-product of genuine love which tears away any mask of self-righteousness. God is the provider of countless blessings which are all too often taken for granted. Lessons in gratitude and humility can only be learned from our good fortunes, while lessons in perseverance and character can only be learned in trials and adversities. Gratitude and humility are closely allied, but are incompatible with hypocrisy and pride. A spirit of gratitude and humility should flow in our thoughts, words and deeds with little conscious awareness.

> I asked God for all things that I may enjoy life
> I was given life that I may enjoy all things
> I am, among all I know, most richly blessed

A spirit of gratitude is of little value unless it is communicated. The following story told by a friend may remind us of someone who may benefit from belated gratitude on our part: Two middle-aged men, Jim and Jack, were discussing their personal and business problems in a city park one Saturday. Jim summed up their chat by saying "There sure isn't much to be thankful for!" Jack thought for a few moments and then replied, "Well, I'm sure grateful to Mrs. Pearson. She was my literature teacher when I was just a kid. She gave me an appreciation of Tennyson which kindled a love of poetry within me. It has remained with me to this very day and gives me much happiness." Jim said, "Did you ever thank her?" Jack paused and reflected on the question and finally said, "No, but I'm going to do it tonight, even after all these years!" That evening two short phone calls identified Mrs. Pearson's current address and Jack sent her a belated note of gratitude.

A couple of weeks later, Jack received the following letter: "My dear Johnny, you will never know how much your letter meant to me. I am a lonely old lady now, widowed and living in a small room. I am able to get along on my pension and can still look after myself and get my meals. Johnny, I taught school for 45 years, and your note is the first letter of appreciation that I ever received. It arrived on a dull, cold morning and it cheered my lonely heart as nothing else has in many years. Thank you from the bottom of my heart. God bless you, Johnny. Yours truly, Mrs. Pearson." This was the beginning of a very special and loving relationship between this elderly lady and her former pupil.

Gentleness and kindness get better results than bluster and fury. The latter harden resistance, but the former melt opposition. Aesop's fable about the sun and the wind is a good illustration. The wind was boasting to the sun that it had greater influence on people. To prove its point, the wind said to the sun, "See that old man over there? I bet I can make him take off his coat sooner than you can!" So the wind blew until it reached a hurricane; but the harder it blew, the tighter the old man wrapped his coat around himself. Finally the wind gave up. Then the sun came out from behind a fleecy cloud and smiled gently on the old man. Presently, he mopped his brow and voluntarily took off his coat. How true to human nature! Kindness and patience are virtues that make all the difference.

God's law is the moral constitution of the universe which is written in our conscience. But the conscience can become dulled and hardened by habitually ignoring God's law. The heart gravitates to those things which we value most. Our first priority in life should be to love God, our second should be to love our fellow man. The more that we make these two priorities a reality in our daily lives, the greater will we experience fulfillment, joy and happiness.

> I sought my soul, but my soul I could not see.
> I sought my God, but my God eluded me.
> I sought my brother, and I found all three.

Unlike man-made laws, the laws of God are timeless and perfect, the Ten Commandments being eternal guidelines for daily living. These living active laws work as surely as the law of gravity. None of us can purposely and habitually break any of these spiritual laws with impunity. The first four commandments define our relationship with God, while the remaining six govern our human relationships.

You and I are free to live as our conscience dictates. Perhaps each one of us should ask ourselves a penetrating question: "If I were put on trial for my moral convictions, would there be enough evidence to convict me?" Individuals with strong moral convictions invariably have a spiritual dimension to their lives. Their beliefs and convictions shape and influence their thoughts, words and deeds. They are not confused by human philosophies or deceived by doctrines that do not recognize God as supreme. They know that truth can never contradict itself and firmly believe that all the treasures of wisdom and understanding are revealed in God's Word.

Chapter III
Perceptions on Success

True success in life can be defined as the pursuit of ideals and goals which benefit others. Success in life is much like a garden — the need to work at it never ends. Every completion should have a new beginning. Great ideas are planted by discerning the lessons and ageless wisdom of the Scriptures. Success is kindled by modeling our character after those who have touched our lives in indelible ways. What we continue to do with the gifts that we possess is the true measure of our success at any particular period in our lives. Successful living is a continuing process of learning, growing, caring and sharing.

We live in a society which worships worldly success. Prestige, distinction, power and wealth are symbols of worldly success which feeds on pride, envy and greed. The pursuit of these symbols of success often becomes the prime purpose in life and an end in itself. Sometimes it is accompanied by a frenzied effort to compete with others, to get ahead and stay ahead. Superficially we may gain a sense of satisfaction and security by wrapping our lives around the pursuit of material goods and pleasures. As time goes on, however, successful living must offer more than self-satisfaction or provide more than temporary escape from boredom. Otherwise a restless feeling of quiet desperation can eventually permeate our lives which cannot be masked by trivial pursuits.

True contentment in life consists not in the abundance of personal possessions but in the fewness of selfish desires. An abundance of goodness is far more important than an abundance of goods. The veneer of worldly success captivates the secular mind and encourages a lifestyle of instant gratification, self-indulgence and consumerism. The affluent lifestyle speaks a clear message of worldly success, giving the illusion of being the sure panacea for all unhappiness. Consequently many individuals allow their lives to be frittered away on frivolous pursuits. The spiritual dimension of their lives becomes irrelevant as they feel no apparent need to trust God for their worldly success.

Self-gratification and self-indulgence are a materialistic form of self-worship. Obsession with immediate sensual gratification is becoming an acceptable part of our lifestyle — love without commitment, rights without responsibilities, getting without giving, self-concern without concern for others. This preoccupation with self-gratification and self-indulgence is called *narcissism*. The term comes from ancient Greek mythology and the story of Narcissus who fell in love with his own image reflected in a stagnant pool of water. Our affluent culture manifests narcissism in countless ways — overt emphasis on sexuality, youthful appearance, luxuries, social and economic status.

The popular concept of success can blind us to our true nature and basic needs as human beings. As we develop a better understanding and perspective of life, we are gradually released from the compulsion to strive for mere temporal accomplishments to gain success. The central principle for a life of significance involves focusing our lives on those values which time does not erase. Love, patience, kindness, goodness, truth, forgiveness, compassion — all of these virtues find their source and ultimate worth in our Creator. All other pursuits should be in harmony with and secondary to these lasting values. Embracing this kind of perspective on life helps one to understand how a humble servant of God like Mother Teresa can be truly more '*successful*' than great celebrities or wealthy tycoons. A little love in the heart can do far more good than a lot of gold in the pocket.

When we choose a well-ordered, simple lifestyle and have an uncomplicated view of life, we are better able to expand the breadth and depth of our inner lives. Externally our lives may not appear significant to the casual observer, but those who know us well can sense an inner peace and contentment that does not depend on the outward trappings of worldly success. From God's perspective, all of us can be successful simply by living a life that is pleasing to Him. Hebrews (Chapter 11) in the New Testament of the Bible describes a number of individuals who

God considered successful. Some were rich, others were poor; a few were famous, but most were unknown; some were in good health, others were in poor health; some lived to an advanced age, others died untimely deaths; all had a simple faith and trust in God.

Our very lifestyle is clearly destroying our future, yet there is no place to hide! We have become blinded and indifferent to an obvious truth — economic growth cannot be sustained indefinitely on our finite planet with its limited resources and single atmosphere shared by all life. Our ever-shrinking global village is subject to the same divine law of *'Cause and Effect'* as that which regulates human relationships. Yet economic growth has become an end in itself and literally defines the word *'progress'* in our affluent society.

Economic growth is inextricably linked to the profit motive which has become not only the measure of success but its very purpose. Quality of life seems to be measured primarily by an ever-higher level of comfort and affluence. The consequences of this worship for growth and affluence as an end in itself are bearing bitter fruit. Our fragile environment is under siege around the globe! Our patterns of living are becoming more and more out of tune with the life-support system of Earth as a whole.

Pollution is the inevitable consequence of the never-ending increase in production and consumption of goods and services. Affluence and pollution are inextricably linked, both driven by an insatiable appetite to *have* more and *consume* more. The most prevalent environmental pollutants are like innumerable threads woven into the very fabric of our consumer-oriented society, making it difficult to remove them without unravelling our many comforts and conveniences. Yet all of us are part of the fragile balance of the total environment and we must share responsibility for its stewardship by preserving it for future generations.

Modern technology has had the effect of shrinking our planet into a global village. The earth's atmosphere is a common resource with no geographical boundaries. Adverse environmental effects cannot be isolated or fully measured as they ripple and seep far and deep. Pollution of the global environment (water, air and soil) has altered the definition of progress from 'standard of living' to the holistic concept of 'quality of life'. The endless pursuit of goods, services, profits and pleasure is playing havoc with our planet's environment. The challenge is greater than merely raising the level of public awareness and consciousness in protecting the environment. Education and legislation may curb the abuse of our environment but they cannot impose a self-sacrificial lifestyle on an affluent society.

Education and good books are no guarantee of good character. Ethics and integrity cannot be turned on and off in either our personal or professional lives. These virtues become part of our being just as character is the sum total of what we are. Ethics and integrity are inseparable and should be learned early in life. They shape conduct and behavior which are the essence of character. Ethical and moral choices are prompted by the conscience which should be kindled and nourished in the early formative years. This inner voice of conscience can be scarred and dulled until its whisper is no longer heard. Over a period of time the conscience can be undermined by a confusing array of situational ethics and moral guidelines.

Our secular society favors a permissive *value-neutral* philosophy which fosters situational ethics. The growing gray area between what is *right* and what is *wrong* is blurred further by legal loopholes and interpretations in the courts. Personal rights are given too much weight at the expense of personal responsibilities — the former are legislated while the latter are largely ignored. Self-gratification and a *me-first* attitude are fostered and promoted in our stiffly competitive, materialistic society. Consequently a growing indifference and cynicism to rules of conduct and behavior have emerged. Laws are enacted in a vain attempt to define the limits of unethical conduct. Paradoxically however, morality can never be legislated into existence. Before temptation can be mastered, a charter of integrity and honesty must first be written in the human heart.

Our permissive culture accepts and promotes the concept that individuals have the right and authority to set their own moral standards and live their own way. The individual has become the final authority over what is right and what is wrong. Personal freedom and civil rights are emphasized and exalted while personal responsibility and accountability have become secondary and incidental. The name of the game is *meology* — if it feels good and you would like to do it, go for it! This indifference to ethics and moral values has consequences beyond measure for individuals and society as a whole.

Greed takes many forms but is frequently masked under the banner of personal rights. As an illustration, there is an increasing tendency to look for a financial remedy to every personal injustice, either real or imagined. No stigma is associated with the filing of frivolous claims, especially when tempted by potentially large awards. Lawyers are sought out who specialize in imaginative reasons for clients to sue. With no fines for making frivolous lawsuits and appeals to the courts, the publicity following successful lawsuits and huge awards generates more frivolous suits.

Some years ago a student sued Columbia University after he flunked out. His lawyer claimed that the university failed to live up to its high standards — to impart character, truth, enlightenment, understanding, justice, honesty, courage, as well as other similar virtues and noble qualities; that the university would develop the whole man, giving him maturity, wisdom and the like. The court dismissed the ridiculous claim, pointing out to the student that the university can lead a horse (or fool) to water but it cannot make him drink.

Ethics courses have achieved curriculum status in many schools of business. Textbooks present traditional philosophies and value systems that can be applied to business practice. But the teaching of business ethics can bring more confusion than clarity when it is couched in relativistic thinking. The idea of universal biblical ethics with accompanying guidelines is considered a myth; consequently no specific system of values is taught to be right. Most influential educators favor situation ethics in which the acceptance of what is right and good is determined by the prevailing culture. Most textbooks have the effect of depersonalizing ethics, leaving personal responsibilities unaddressed.

Moral values and ethics are caught more than they are taught. College is too late to teach ethics to students who already have their own standard of values. The most that college courses in ethics can do is to make students more aware of the reasons underlying moral principles. Ethics courses, however, cannot realistically claim to make students morally better. Ethics and values must come before and reach out beyond mere learning. Even Albert Einstein (1879-1955), one of our greatest scientists, believed that every student should possess an understanding for personal values and the morally good.

Organizations maintaining the highest ethical standards are those where individual responsibility and personal integrity are emphasized and recognized. The examples set by leaders in organizations are crucial in creating a positive climate. Codes of conduct outline the creed of a company, expressing recognition of responsibility and the conduct through which that responsibility is fulfilled. Each individual in the organization has a responsibility depending on his position to uphold the company's creed and stand liable for his conduct. This is in sharp contrast to most organizations where ethical ambiguity is the rule of the work place.

Schools, colleges and universities are generational way stations that give us a glimpse of our future society. The objective of these institutions should be not just to educate students in specific disciplines but to open and nourish young minds in pursuit of self-reliance and truth. The focus of learning should be a better understanding of oneself and a greater capacity for sound judgment. Institutions of learning are composed of individuals — administrators, teachers, professors and students. These individuals are an important cross-section of society at large, and if our educational institutions are misguided it is because society at large has lost its way. Education at its best points the way to personal fulfillment, self-reliance and true success in life. It molds us as individuals because education in its broadest sense occurs everywhere, not just in the classroom.

Education in its fullest sense cannot be divorced from the consideration of God as the ultimate Author of all truth. Our secular society is adrift on the awful sea of human folly, substituting human opinion for the basic textbook on true education, the Bible. Secularism has its own implicit values and selfish priorities, its own worldly gods and faiths. A child miseducated is a child lost but true education leads to a productive life. The home must rank as the primary source of education, yet many parents abdicate their crucial responsibilities. Consequently many schools have become more like crisis centers than educational institutions. Paradoxically knowledge is increasing at a bewildering pace yet living a meaningful life has become more challenging.

Although manmade laws are necessary in every society, they are somewhat like the cages in a zoo — they may restrain serious wrongdoing and keep it from getting out of hand but they cannot change the basic nature of the human heart. Vice and crime flow from bad character rather than stemming primarily from economic or social status. Irresponsible parental upbringing is the root cause of many mixed-up adolescents becoming involved in drugs and crime. A sense of 'what is right and what is wrong' must be taught in the home before it can be taught effectively in the schools. Christian family values are the institutional bulwark that shape personal character and moral choices.

The truth of the adage *'an ounce of prevention is worth a pound of cure'* seems to be lost in the rising tide of crime. Personal moral choices and behavior are influenced by the conscience which is shaped early in life. Violence and crime are not symptoms of a disease or illness, nor is sociological background the root cause. The adverse effects of drug, alcohol and other substance abuse should be part of a pre-kindergarten program in the home. It is somewhat late to focus on imprisoning drug users, producers and sellers which require more and more prisons, treatment centers and police. The influence and restraint of God's laws on the heart and the conscience are far superior to any manmade laws or prisons.

Education is a multi-faceted continuing process that begins at birth. Infants are taught and their character is shaped from the time they leave their mothers' womb. Babies watch their parents, listen to the tone of their voice, and pick up their attitude about countless things — love, patience, kindness, music, books, etc. The first few years are the crucial formative ones when parents have the greatest impact on shaping the character of their children. As children reach school age, parents must realize that schools are only *one* element in their continual education. Many well-meaning parents work hard and sacrifice much for their children but they abdicate responsibility for shaping their values and character. The consequences of parental indifference and neglect can bear bitter fruit during the teenage years — school dropouts, pregnancy, drugs, smoking, alcohol.

The development of skills is the primary objective of our educational institutions. It is too much to expect grade schools to teach good character, ethics and morals to students who start with none at home. The Bible repeatedly and consistently stresses the parental role in education. Responsible parents need not be scholars to mold the character and values of their offspring. The book of Proverbs is essentially an instruction manual written by a wise father to his children. It contains literally a gold mine of guidance and counseling for all parents.

Education at its best teaches true values — a sense of meaning and moral direction to life and the way to truly successful living. Sound education teaches that all things are a matter of cause and effect. It teaches the consequences of wrong living as well as the rewards of right living. Schools must not succumb to humanist philosophy which does not recognize a higher authority than man. Humanists promote the concept of a world with logic, reason and science holding the keys to understanding and solution to all problems.

The essence of education at its best is a continual process of mental growth and development in virtuous ways. The worth of our youth should not be measured by scholastic achievements alone, nor should success in a career be measured primarily by accumulation of wealth. Our youth should make their own career choices, with personal satisfaction and opportunity to grow professionally taking priority over monetary rewards. Wise career decisions require self-knowledge of special talents, aptitudes and interests. Skills can be acquired but interests are inherent and the key to job satisfaction.

Parents who lack any knowledge of God's Word find it difficult to explain the meaning and purpose of life to their children. The Bible is the character of God in print and parents have a vital role in revealing God's character to their children. A sense of strong moral direction is given to their lives when children are taught from a bedrock of truth. Manmade regulations are based on shifting opinions rather than unchanging convictions. Parental guidance based on God's Word has influence and authority far beyond mere human opinion!

The quality of education should be measured by the product that our schools are turning out rather than by the amount of money spent. Parents and teachers alike tend to focus on academic achievements alone.

The worth of children as human beings should not be measured solely by their grades. In elementary schools particularly, teaching ethics and building character should be an integral part of the curriculum. Values, like vices, are planted at an early age. Education without values can be misguided and should be opposed as strongly as drug use. Teacher-competency examinations should be encouraged and recognized as standard procedure for merit rating, recognition and promotion.

News never defines itself! Unlike beauty or goodness, news is in the eye of the creator rather than the beholder. News is a human creation that often reveals as much about its makers as it does about its subjects. Unlike the printed media, television has the unchallenged power to literally define the news to a captive audience of passive spectators. TV network news is essentially a collection of capsuled stories about society rather than being its mirror. It masquerades as a mirror of authority for defining the news for its viewers. Dramatic, sensational or conversational events tend to dominate TV news, with the prime concern being to fascinate or entertain rather than to educate. TV news clips and sound bites tend to create a distorted image of what is happening in the world around us.

The television world is becoming the basis for many of our beliefs and values as a society. Repeated viewing of similar kinds of programs has an effect on our imagination, our learning pattern and even our behavior. Without any conscious awareness our value system is affected by excessive or indiscriminate viewing of television. Perceptions of reality rather than reality itself influence conduct and behavior, particularly on young children with impressionable minds. Much of the influence of television is negative, especially on young children who cannot distinguish fantasy from reality. They tend to mimic individuals who are their role models, many of whom are characters from television programs. Young and old alike are exposed to a *'junk-food'* mental diet of television which feeds on spiritual stagnation and mental malnutrition.

Television fosters a passive, consumer mentality. Most commercially-sponsored programs are superficially entertaining, living or dying by their viewer ratings. Television possesses a seductive fascination that exerts a kind of psychological spell even when programs are utter drivel. Its appeal lies in the very nature of the medium whereby another world can be summoned into our living room merely by pressing a button. Commercial television rarely rises above mediocre levels to stimulate the mind of the viewer. It has become a tool for promoting many products and services of dubious value through misleading and exaggerated advertisements. Fortunately, publicly-sponsored quality programs are becoming more readily available which nurture and educate thoughtful minds rather than merely entertain — musical classics, wildlife/nature documentaries, etc.

Regulated, selective viewing of quality television can be beneficial to children and adolescents. It can stimulate language development, visual and auditory skills, as well as curiosity about science and geography. On the other hand, indiscriminate or excessive viewing can be devastating to young impressionable minds. The graphic display of crime and violence is all too prevalent on commercial channels. Television viewing can be mesmerizing, blotting out the real world and making viewers mentally passive. Young viewers can become susceptible to whatever the 'idiot box' sends their way, lapping up messages of corruption, intrigue, infidelity and violence. Images are transmitted that remain deeply imprinted on young impressionable minds. The increasing amount of violence and obscenity is undermining traditional family values and the moral fiber of our youth. The consequences of this steady erosion of ethics and values are far reaching. Unfortunately, quality educational TV programs that encourage follow-up reading by young viewers are rare indeed.

Moderation is a continuing challenge as it requires perception, judgment and discipline. Any good thing if carried to excess can be counterproductive and even harmful. For example, there is the wife who is so involved in church-related activities that she loses touch with her husband and becomes indifferent to his concerns and needs. Or the pastor who is so involved with his parishioners and their problems that he neglects those of his family; or the spendthrift who is lavish with his money to the point that he is irresponsible; or the penny-pincher who loves his money so much he cannot part with any of it; or the workaholic who is so wrapped up with his job that he neglects his family; or the devoted mother who gives her only child so much love and attention that neither is contented whenever they are apart. These illustrations demonstrate how an obsession, even with a noble cause, can be self-defeating and leads to tunnel vision.

Where our treasure is, there our heart will be also! Our lifestyle reveals our values and priorities which affect and often govern our important decisions. Our thoughts, our efforts and our time are captured by those things which are important to us. What we do and how we act in our daily lives are influenced by our priorities and values. Time cannot be stored or retrieved even in this age of the computer. We can resolve today to make our lives more fulfilling and rewarding. Today is the first day of the rest of our lives. Today well-lived makes a happy memory of yesterday and a vision of hope for tomorrow.

Daydreams are often goals in the early formative stages. We should set goals that are beyond our immediate grasp, yet not out of sight. They should be action-oriented targets that can be defined, visualized and committed to writing. Our goals need to dominate our thoughts and then they become our priorities. Specific written goals are the tools which make purpose achievable because purpose is the engine that powers our lives. Short-range goals are the stepping stones to long-range purpose. We must be true to ourselves in having meaningful goals in life by following our convictions and our conscience.

It is not easy to articulate important goals that give purpose and direction to our lives. Thinking vaguely about long-term goals is not the same as writing them down. Unwritten goals usually remain nebulous while written goals tend to be more concrete and specific. Valuable new perspectives can be gained by translating thoughts to paper where they can be closely examined. Goals take on greater meaning and value when they are given life in print. Written goals, however, should never be carved in stone; periodically they should be reviewed — analyzed, refined, changed, updated.

At different stages in our lives, goals and priorities change. We should interpret and evaluate our goals from the perspective of what will be important to us in the future. An initial list of lifetime goals is usually general in nature and could include such topics as career, family, success, love, happiness. General lifetime goals can be made more specific by asking ourselves how we would like to spend the next five years of our lives. Priorities can then be attached to these specific goals by asking ourselves how we would spend our time if we knew that we would die suddenly six months hence.

Signs of an eroded value system include substituting peace of mind and a clear conscience for selfish gain, failing to distinguish *needs* from *wants*, and having the 'making of money' the prime objective in life. However, responsible financial planning is beneficial for living within a budget and minimizing waste and extravagance. Greater peace of mind, freedom from financial stress, and greater self-confidence for getting debt-free are important by-products of financial planning.

Nothing is wrong with possessing money and things as long as they do not possess us. The more that selfish pride is fed, the greater is the hunger inside. Obsessions with money and what money can buy often mask much deeper needs. Money and material possessions can fascinate and even excite us but as time passes they take on less and less importance in our lives. Material things do not give lasting satisfaction but eventually can leave us longing for something more that is missing in our lives. The human soul craves for a certain peace and serenity that remain elusive as long as God remains a total stranger to us.

Where our treasure is, there our heart will be also (Matt. 6:21). Material success and possessions are not bad in themselves, but rather the underlying attitudes of envy, greed and the love of money. Unfortunately, many people have the mistaken impression that more money and more things automatically mean more happiness. This mirage is cultivated by our modern society with its emphasis on materialistic values. Skillful advertising and promotional techniques create the urge for 'impulse buying' even if it means going into debt. Consumers are urged to buy now and pay later, with the result that many individuals and families find themselves drifting deeper and deeper into debt.

Self-confidence and self-esteem are increased by establishing goals that are both realistic and challenging. It is necessary to realize what problems are involved in order to achieve our goals but it is important that we do not become easily discouraged. Perseverance strengthens character and we should never be afraid of failure in pursuing any worthwhile goal. Every challenging and rewarding goal is necessarily beyond our immediate grasp. The strength of character gained far outweighs any temporary sacrifices. The type of goals and priorities which we set for ourselves reflect our moral and spiritual values.

An illustration of pursuing a wrong goal with disastrous consequences concerns a star football player named Davis. It was a sudden-death playoff game and his team was winning by a close score with just seconds remaining in the game. The other team had the ball at mid-field. Suddenly the ball was fumbled and Davis scooped it up. He evaded one tackler, then another! The third tackler spun Davis around but could not bring him down! David twisted free, leaped over another tackler and broke into the open field. He glanced behind to see players of both teams in hot pursuit. The home crowd was in a frenzy, its roar drowning out the desperate shouts of his teammates as he crossed the goal line "Stop, Davis, stop! You're going the wrong way!" Davis triumphantly held the ball high above his head and then jubilantly threw it to the fans. A hush came over the crowd as a teammate sadly put his arm around Davis' shoulder and told him that he had lost the game by going the wrong way. How true to life! In our eager pursuit of worldly goals, many of us do not hear HIS voice saying to us, "I am the Way, the Truth and the Life" (John 14:6).

It is never too late (or too soon) to strive for a worthy goal. Setting challenging goals plays a vital part in successful living. A good feeling of self-esteem comes from making a commitment to achieve a worthwhile goal. Our personal values and priorities determine the kind of objectives that we set for ourselves. Any worthwhile goal by its very nature requires effort and perseverance. All that we need is the self-discipline to do what is necessary to realize our objectives. The strength of character gained in the pursuit of a worthwhile goal far outweighs any sacrifices. Achievements that involve little effort are of little consequence.

Most young people want their lives to be both meaningful and rewarding. Unfortunately many are not committed to any challenging goals, and consequently become discontented as they search for meaning and purpose. Some may change their jobs to obtain temporary relief from boredom. Others may seek temporary diversions which relieve the symptoms but not the cause of boredom. Unfortunately, prolonged boredom particularly among young people can lead to unhealthy diversions such as drugs, alcohol, gambling and overeating. They have become victims of boredom due to the absence of any challenging personal goals to occupy their thoughts and channel their energy. The diligent pursuit of worthwhile goals satisfies the natural craving in all of us for a sense of self-worth and accomplishment. In pursuing any goal, regardless of our age, we should strive to make ourselves useful to others. In so doing, we will bring some measure of happiness to others which in turn gives us a greater sense of self-worth.

Patient thought and sustained concentration in the pursuit of a worthwhile endeavor have the same effect as a magnifiying glass focusing the gentle rays of the sun on a single point. The intensity can be so great as to kindle a fire. Isaac Newton required long periods of unbroken concentration to discover the underlying principle which explained the law of gravitation. The great scientist deliberated over a mass of accumulated data and calculations for endless hours, day-in and day-out with little personal regard for time or nourishment. Finally he came up with a simple mathematical formula to explain the attraction of bodies in relation to their masses and distances between them. Even a brilliant scientist like Newton required perseverance and sustained concentration to discover one of God's laws of the universe.

Without faith there can be no perseverance, for perseverance is the test of our faith. Perseverance means doing tough upstream things first, and looking downstream for future rewards. Spiritual faith is not just belief in God but believing that we are an integral part of God's plan. Creative imagination, self-esteem, values and self-reliance are fostered by this kind of faith. Faith in action seems like a miracle to losers in the arena of life. Having little or no perseverance of their own, they are losers by default rather than defeat. Every great winner in life would be a loser without faith and perseverance. Everyone wants success but few are willing to pay the price — persistence!

An effective technique for realizing a worthwhile goal is to vividly picture it in our mind. This mental process should be repeated frequently until the image is firmly fixed and sinks deeply into the subconscious mind. The seedling is nourished whenever the goal dominates our thoughts and time. Astonishing results can be realized as untapped resources are released to overcome obtacles in realizing the goal. When one worthwhile goal is realized, more self-confidence and a greater feeling of self-worth are gained to set other goals that are even more challenging. When we commit to the Lord whatever we do, our plans *will* surely succeed (Prov. 16:3).

Making tough decisions can be stressful — so stressful in fact, that there is a tendency to procrastinate indefinitely. But time and events often make tough decisions for us; making no decision is really a decision to do nothing. Indecision can be destructive when fear and uncertainty are dominant. When confronted with two courses of action in a complex major decision, the right course is usually revealed by weighing all the arguments pro and con for each. While this approach may seem amazingly simple, it is highly effective and reliable in arriving at right decisions.

Making important decisions is an essential part of personal growth and development, presenting opportunities and valuable lessons to learn from past mistakes. Seeking wise counsel can supplement but should never supplant the pros and cons for each course of action. Confidence and experience are gained as decision-making ability becomes more successful and personally rewarding. Risking time and effort pursuing worthwhile goals is a risk well taken.

The mental picture which we have of ourselves is called self-image. When properly nourished and cultivated, self-image is a primary source from which success grows. When neglected however, our self-image can become a spawning pond for bad behavior and underachievement. Healthy self-esteem is the basis for our ability to love others and pursue worthwhile goals. We are the sum total of our thoughts, attitudes and actions. Self-acceptance is the key to developing healthy self-esteem.

There is too much emphasis in the news media on those things that are wrong with our world. History demonstrates that for any particular period we can perceive the best or the worst of times, depending on what we want to see. The good old days are here and now if only we will look for them. Every generation has its own problems and laments its own crises. Only the nature of problems and challenges change from one generation to another. We should adapt to change by viewing problems as opportunities, and stumbling blocks as stepping-stones. Since change is inevitable, we should look forward to the promise of each new day and discover that the good old days are here and now. Having an optimistic perspective on life enables us to see goodness in the world more clearly.

Where our treasure is, there our heart will be also (Matthew 6:21). How we see life truly makes all the difference in measuring success in life. Honesty and integrity are prime virtues of successful living, character and personal values setting us apart. True success embraces the philosophy that an abundance of goodness far surpasses an abundance of goods. Life does not consist merely in the abundance of possessions (Luke 12:15). The only treasures which are truly ours are those we lay up in the hearts of others. The seeds of greatness lie within each one of us, waiting and begging to be nourished through the pursuit of lofty goals and ideals which benefit others and are pleasing to God. All Scripture is the Word of God which thoroughly equips us for good works (2 Timothy 3:16,17).

Chapter IV
Perceptions on Marriage

Every happy marriage is a partnership in love. The greatest marriage manual in print, the Bible, calls upon us to *'do unto others as we would have them do unto us!'* The Biblical definition of love is clear and devoid of any ambiguity: "Love is patient, love is kind. It does not envy, it does not boast, it is not proud. It is not rude, it is not self-seeking, it is not easily angered, it keeps no record of wrongs. Love does not delight in evil but rejoices with the truth. It always protects, always trusts, always hopes, always perseveres. Love never fails." (1 Cor. 13). In contrast to popular notions of physical attraction only, love is an expression of deep appreciation for another human being. During the romantic phase of a marital relationship, feelings of excitement, bliss and ecstasy dominate. However, as those fires temper with each passing year a happy marriage must develop a special husband/wife friendship that grows rather than succumbs with time. This special *friendship* is a rare treasure but ultimately it proves to be the most rewarding aspect of any marriage. Both lives are twice blessed through sharing hopes and disappointments, joys and sorrows, triumphs and tragedies.

Love thrives on thoughtfulness but withers with indifference and neglect. Love should never be rationed or withheld as it craves for daily expression. Both husband and wife should guard against taking each other for granted. Empathy is having sensitivity to the needs of the other, which is an invisible thread that weaves a lasting fabric in every happy marriage. This empathy should grow deeper with time and enrich the marital relationship. Mutual respect and trust are constant companions in this partnership of love. Separate or divergent interests should never be a serious threat to a successful marriage; short times that spouses are apart should only increase their joy of being together. Neither time nor distance should threaten an enduring marital relationship.

Marriage should be a serious commitment not to be entered into or wriggled out of lightly! The consequences of unhappy marriages are often lost in statistics — divorces, single parents, foster homes, correctional institutions and the like. There are no reliable statistics for counting the marriages that become endurance contests where husband and wife are practically strangers living under the same roof. Paradoxically, many couples do a much better job in planning their careers and investment portfolios than in their marital relationships. The institution of marriage is no longer recognized as a lifelong commitment in a permissive society which promotes self-centeredness and instant gratification. This cult of *'meology'* cripples commitment, making it easy to wriggle out of *'disposable'* marriages.

Intimacy in a marriage does not happen on the wedding night but grows slowly over a lifetime. Unfortunately many marriages end before the process of intimacy really begins. It is the missing dimension in too many marriages — the gradual process of becoming one, not just in body but in mind and spirit. The all-inclusive word that defines intimacy is *sharing*, which is much more than sex. Intimacy gives meaning to sex, but sex does not create intimacy. Giving through sharing is the expression of true love which is the catalyst that binds every happy marriage. Intimacy grows rather than stagnates with time. It is the priceless experience of sharing two lives together — the joys and the sorrows, the laughter and the tears, the triumphs and the trials. With God at the center of an intimate marriage, love radiates daily in countless little ways.

Happy couples know instinctively that love can be returned only when it is freely given. This simple but profound truth is the cornerstone of their marital relationship. They know deep down in their hearts that love and gratitude are inseparable, and that both are as indispensable to their happiness as the very air they breathe. The true spirit of love and gratitude flows from the heart with little conscious awareness. The best lessons in gratitude are learned from recognizing and appreciating good fortunes and daily blessings.

Genuine love is a process that grows deeper with time. An unselfish, giving and caring atmosphere is fostered through an intensive awareness of each partner's needs and longings. Living through difficulties together, far from being a burden, draws husband and wife even closer in a committed marriage. Tolerance, patience and thoughtfulness are nourished and demonstrated in countless little ways. Even with best intentions, however, one spouse may behave badly at times toward the other, but should never be reluctant to say two important words 'I'm sorry' and really mean them. A sincere apology has the effect of melting even the hardest heart and purging ill-feeling in the process. The sin of foolish selfish pride should never be allowed to become a stumbling block in a healthy marital relationship.

Often we do not show our loved ones as much courtesy or consideration as we routinely accord casual acquaintances. Day-in, day-out contact with our spouse tends to breed indifference. The heart of a sincere apology should be the intention not to repeat the mistake. When there is no regret, the stage is set for repeating the same type of mistake. The common tendency to make excuses dilutes the effectiveness of an apology and deprives the other spouse of a chance to be forgiving. A direct no-excuses apology leaves both husband and wife feeling better about themselves even though one spouse may be primarily at fault. Accepting an apology can be just as important a social skill as delivering an apology — some small gesture can cement the bond of forgiveness.

Many couples think their domestic life would be happier if only they had a better home, lived in a different neighborhood or had a better job. This was the attitude of one middle-aged couple, Jane and Jim, who quarreled violently over trivial matters. Each blamed the other for starting their quarrels, and domestic stress finally built up to the breaking point. One day in desperation, Jane found herself opening the door to an empty church. As she sat in a pew meditating and praying, God became very real to her for the first time in years. In God's presence she began to realize that she was just as aloof and spiteful as her husband. Jane earnestly prayed for God's grace and strength before leaving.

That evening when her husband came home he was more exhausted and irritable than usual. After dinner, while still sitting at the table, Jane summoned up the courage to say, "Jim, I'm sorry that our marriage is such a mess. It's all my fault." There was astonishment on Jim's face! For a whole minute, which seemed like a lifetime to his wife, he just looked at her and finally said, "What do you mean?" His wife responded by recounting many of the nasty things that she had said and done. She explained how her self-righteous attitude had made her feel that all their marital problems were *his* fault, but now she realized that she was even more to blame. Jim got up from his chair, came around the table, lifted his wife from her chair and put his arms around her. He asked forgiveness for all the hurtful things he had said and done to her.

That night they rediscovered a very deep love and tenderness that they had not known for years. Previously their spiritual lives were stagnant, but now they grew closer to God and thanked Him daily for their many blessings. As each day, week and month passed, Jane wanted to do more and more for Jim. Surprisingly she found that the more she did for him, the more he in turn did for her. *True love* always trusts, always hopes, always perseveres; *true love* never fails.

The power of love, like the power of electricity is invisible but just as real. Few of us understand how electric power is generated, harnessed and transmitted, but we know from experience that it works and makes our lives more enjoyable. But like so many other blessings, we tend to take it for granted until we lose it. Unlike electricity, however, love never fails.

The amazing power of love is unlimited and miraculously *increases* the more it is shared with others. Love cannot be conserved or stored like electricity for emergencies but craves for daily outpouring, sharing and expression. Love can be returned only when it is freely given. Love thrives on thoughtfulness and kindness but withers with indifference and neglect.

Physical sexual expression is a very complex relationship involving the deepest self-expression of two individuals of the opposite sex. It is never a morally neutral act but is either right or wrong. Its very nature and purpose involves a growth process that requires a degree of openness and trust that can only be found within the marital relationship. Sex is used and abused by both the electronic and printed media to sell everything from soap to automobiles. The subtle power of suggestion conditions many adolescents and youth to sexual permissiveness and immorality. Too often the media and entertainment industry present premarital sex as a noble experience, extramarital encounters as healthy, and homosexual or bisexual behavior as acceptable. When sexual intercourse is not an act of marital love, it can be emotionally, phychologically and physically destructive. Sexual abstinence before marriage and sexual faithfulness within marriage is the best defense against all sexually transmitted diseases.

Many misconceptions exist about sex that can cause serious problems between husbands and wives. Traditionally, boys and girls have been taught to conform to certain gender roles — girls should be demure and passive, boys should be macho and aggressive. When girls become adults and marry, many feel that they should still be passive and conceal their true sexual feelings and needs. In fact, most healthy women equal or even exceed men in their sexual needs and desires. The best sex occurs when both husband and wife just let things happen without either being preoccupied with sexual performance. The pleasure and fulfilment of each partner are heightened when both respond emotionally to stimulation and communicate their mutual enjoyment. Unfortunately popular culture exalts sex to unrealistic expectations. Consequently many couples feel inadequate and anxious which inhibits their sexual relations.

Communication breakdown can be a serious problem within the intimacy of marriage. As it is not uncommon for husbands and wives to have differing levels of sexual desire, it is vital that both spouses have loving communication and understanding. Physical affection is an important part of an intimate relationship and should never be rationed regardless of the frequency of sexual relations. Hurtful words, criticism or indifference by either husband or wife makes it very difficult to have a healthy sexual relationship. Both partners treasure expressions of tenderness and thoughtfulness as they want to feel needed and special.

Effective communication between husband and wife is essential for a good sexual relationship. It means detecting feelings and little clues that may reveal more than mere words. Most wives want tenderness and romance, with little thoughtful gestures to show that their husbands really care about them. However, many wives have some false assumptions about their husbands' wants and needs, many of which are not considered masculine macho traits. Most husbands react positively to loving, tender assertiveness by their wives. On the other hand, the husband welcomes the occasional sexual initiative by his wife as it makes him feel cherished and wanted. Wives often hesitate to initiate any overtures, being fearful either of putting pressure on their husbands or worrying about being rejected. In a good sexual relationship, wives and husbands alike should be willing to take some initiative.

The highest expression of human communication should be the husband/wife relationship. Happy couples freely express their feelings to each other, especially when one spouse feels troubled or depressed. Unexpressed problems fester with time and can undermine an otherwise good marriage. Strained communications can affect all important areas of a marital relationship including putting a damper on sharing common interests and activities, even sexual relations. In a healthy marital relationship, both partners are able to freely verbalize their thoughts and feelings. Sometimes the best expression of love can be a sympathetic ear, a silent caring presence, a gentle touch, or just an understanding glance.

The practice of freely showing feelings and emotional needs reflects a healthy marital relationship. The honesty and openness of disclosing innermost thoughts and feelings is an expression of trust and love. In general, husbands have more difficulty talking about their feelings and emotions than do their wives. Real communication develops when both are sensitive to each other's feelings and can also articulate their own feelings. Little non-verbal clues and an attentive ear comprise the other basic ingredients for real communication. Many unnecessary marital battles occur as a result of poorly encoded and decoded messages. Even the tone of voice and inflection of words can convey right or wrong meaning.

Sometimes a marriage can degenerate to the point where the only communication is done with spiteful remarks. On other occasions, one or both spouses may pull into their shell and sever all communication. As time goes on they drift further and further apart until they literally become strangers under the same roof. By contrast, couples with a healthy relationship realize the importance of developing and maintaining a positive emotional climate. When one spouse seems worried or a little depressed, the other demonstrates empathy and concern by being *'emotional blotting paper'* for unburdening problems. Usually the wife is better than the husband in assuming the role of *'chief climate-maker'* as she tends to be more sensitive and attuned to emotions.

Empathy is one of the key ingredients to effective communication — it is *'feeling with'* which is much more than *'feeling for'* another person. Empathy involves trying to put ourselves in the other individual's shoes so that we can better understand what the other person is going through. We can practice empathy by being more open and sensitive to the needs of those near and dear to us. By looking for the good in others, we are communicating love which is one message that we all need. Empathy is ever conscious of the fact that individuals are not always on the same wavelength, often hear a different drummer and see things through a different lens. Empathy is understanding that people can see the same scene from different viewpoints, depending on what is important to them. Love is an active rather than a passive or static emotion. Love looks for and finds *value* and *good* in another person even when it is not evident. In a loving relationship, one touch is worth a thousand words (with one exception — *I love you*). Love involves faith and letting go of fear. We cannot freely give love unless we feel love within.

Good listeners learn a great deal but chatterboxes learn very little. In the communicating process, knowledge is not always wisdom nor is sympathy always understanding. Listening for truth and speaking the truth means being perceptive, and not letting ads or fads make us victims of distortions or self-indulgence.

The art of good listening can only enrich any marital relationship. Good listening acknowledges the importance of our spouse by detecting feelings as well as hearing what is said. The underlying cause of poor communication is insufficient caring and empathy by one or both partners. Any deceptive game of pretending is a poor substitute for genuine interest in what is said. A little good listening goes a long way in deepening any marital relationship. At times it is necessary to sense troubled feelings of our spouse which cannot easily be articulated — the real message that is spoken or sometimes unspoken can often be missed.

The power of the attentive ear can be awesome. In a close husband/wife relationship, each partner is able to read between the lines and pick up little clues which may reveal a deep but unexpressed need. In many marriages, it is not uncommon to hear only the words spoken and miss the real message. In some instances, preconceived opinions or conclusions by one spouse can hinder and even sever lines of communication. A good listener does not interrupt or disturb the silence merely to command attention, but strives to understand the real meaning behind the words spoken. A silent caring presence is often the best expression of love, for there is always a time for words but also a time for silence. Silence can often be the best response, especially when words are inadequate to express our inner thoughts and deepest feelings.

In every marriage, there are times when one spouse does not feel loving toward the other. But sudden lack of affection may be due to a temporary mood or an underlying problem. Regardless of the cause, there are two important questions that should be asked by the other spouse. "Have I done something wrong?" If the answer is reassuring, the other question should be asked, "Is there anything I can do?" Communication breakdown is a serious problem in all human relationships but especially within the intimacy of marriage. The bonds in any marriage are strengthened when both partners are good listeners. Effective communication in marriage implies not only hearing the words spoken but also getting the real message. It means being able to detect feelings and watch for little clues that may reveal more than mere words. Messages are often passed that need no words between husband and wife, especially when deep feelings cannot be articulated easily.

Even in a healthy loving marriage, some conflict is as inevitable as the sunrise. However, there is a crucial difference in the way disagreements are handled. In an unstable marriage, hostility is often hurled directly at the spouse in personal barbs. Vicious verbal combat is extremely damaging to any relationship when the avowed purpose is to deeply hurt the partner. By contrast, the occasional healthy disagreement focuses on the issue without any personal barbs that could damage the ego of either spouse. In a good marriage, both husband and wife realize that anger and resentment only fester in silence. Most couples can enhance their relationship and improve communication by identifying and neutralizing any trigger points that cause anger.

Any meaningful relationship in a marriage requires good communication and empathy. Most arguments can be diffused by keeping in mind that there is usually some grain of truth in differing points of view. By acknowledging this fact without equivocation, abusive arguments can be disarmed before they begin. Responding with patience and empathy rather than impulsively may not be easy when an emotional or controversial issue arises, but the rewards of a congenial marital relationship are many times greater than winning any argument.

Financial problems can undermine a stable marriage and cause worry and stress for both husband and wife. Responsible management of money begins by recognizing that all expenditures fall into one of two categories — needs or wants. A *need* is a biological necessity such as basic food, clothing and shelter. A *want* is a desire set in motion by no basic necessity. In practice, credit should seldom, if ever, be used to satisfy a want. The eager anticipation of possessing a wanted item is often greater than the pleasure of having it. Financial bondage is the result of wrong priorities and lack of financial responsibility rather than inadequate income. The wise individual learns to live *with* credit rather than *by* it. Credit is much like alcohol in many ways — it is easy to get hooked on if not used wisely and in moderation.

Increased harmony in the home and greater peace of mind flow from responsible financial planning. This requires a budget, which is a systematic method of living within our income. Credit is a trust relationship, but many couples live within their credit rather than within their income. No effort should be spared to evade deadly credit traps that rob so many couples of their financial freedom. The irresponsible use of credit is an abuse of credit which leads to worry and financial bondage. Instant credit encourages impulse buying which can lead to living beyond our means. Credit cards should be used only as a convenience, never as a necessity. The credit habit should be avoided for all consumer goods as it undermines the effectiveness of a family budget. An effective way of eliminating a common source of indebtedness is to use *'plastic surgery'* on all credit cards except one, which should be used solely for convenience purposes but never because funds are insufficient.

In every marriage, love thrives on thoughtfulness but withers with neglect. A dull marriage can wither and grow stale, eventually suffering from dry rot. Everything may look fine externally, but any fun and light-heartedness can gradually disappear through neglect or default. A spirit of fun is crucial in any fulfilling relationship. Every married couple should never be so busy or serious that fun is no longer a priority. Fun can take many forms — setting aside a regular evening each week for a date alone, a thoughtful surprise that is pleasing to your spouse, or some activity that reflects shared values and interests. Although marriage thrives on familiarity and routine, the relationship also needs a sparkle now and then to keep it from going stale.

A good sense of humor can enrich any marriage. Wives who want to try a new recipe on their husbands may find the following cooking analogy helpful. Some women keep their husbands constantly in hot water, others freeze them, a few put them in a stew, and the odd one keeps them in a pickle. Such husbands cannot be expected to be good and tender nor to last very long! On the other hand, wives who really love their husbands add a little sugar and spice, butter them up, stirring ever so gently until tender and delicious. These wives invariably find their husbands enticingly agreeable but more important, well preserved!

True forgiveness is the acid test of genuine love; it does not harbor resentment by keeping a mental record of wrongs. A legalistic attitude by either spouse can undermine an otherwise healthy marital relationship. A husband prayed long and earnestly after he learned of his wife's unfaithfulness that threatened to break up his home, until finally a spirit of forgiveness overflowed from his heart. He went directly to his safety deposit box and removed a pack of letters which contained irrefutable evidence of his wife's infidelity. In any court of law this evidence would definitely set him free with no legal obligations whatever to his unfaithful wife. But he was directed by a power beyond himself to cast the letters into the fire. As the evidence went up in smoke, all means of getting even with his wife disappeared. In true forgiveness, the bitter evidence was consumed with fire and transformed into ashes. His heavy burden of bitterness and resentment melted away. Now he was free at last — free to blot out the smoldering resentment of the past and heal the festering wounds in his marriage. True forgiveness is a powerful antidote for bitterness, anger and resentment. It liberates both the forgiver and the forgiven as great healing powers are set in motion. Love is the power behind true forgiveness.

In a truly happy marriage, empathy permeates all areas of the husband/wife relationship — each having a deep feeling for and feeling with the other. As their love grows deeper, so does their empathy as they become more thoughtful, considerate and sensitive to each other's feelings and needs. They look for and find *value* and *good* in each other even when it is not clearly evident. Both partners feel free to expose their inadequacies, confident that they will be accepted. From mutual acceptance grows mutual trust and respect, both partners accepting the other for what they are and not betraying that trust. As each spouse develops special esteem for the other, their relationship takes on a rare quality of closeness and intimacy. In this kind of relationship, each partner makes the other feel that they are the most important person in the world.

Happy couples communicate in depth by learning to express their feelings freely in contrast to harboring ill feelings. They learn to avoid any habits or traits which obviously annoy each other. They realize that some things can be relatively minor to one spouse but a constant aggravation to the other. In those situations, only common sense dictates that the source of aggravation should be dealt with rather than ignored. Thoughtfulness and kindness toward each other is ever present but they resist any temptation to try to change each other. Happy couples cultivate the art of knowing how and when to compromise, avoiding any self-righteous legalistic attitude in their relationship. They freely admit their shortcomings to each other and keep no mental record of the other's wrongs, either real or imaginary. Above all, they never break faith with their partner for they know that a shattered trust can leave permanent scars.

Brian and Ruth have all the important qualities for a happy marriage. They are just naturally thoughtful and considerate of each other, whether alone or with friends. On a recent occasion a guest at a dinner party took Brian aside and asked him the secret of his happy marriage. Brian confided that the early years of his marriage were rough. In fact at one stage he and Ruth were ready to call it quits. Then one Thanksgiving Sunday they decided to attend church for the first time since they were married. There was no particular part of the service that had a great impact on either of them, yet they left the church with a new spirit.

When Brian and Ruth got home they decided to do something very unusual. Each made a list of all the things they *didn't* like about the other. Brian recalled that his list was longer than Ruth's. Then they exchanged lists. To their surprise, things appeared on each list that were never openly discussed or shared, while some things were on neither list that were fully expected. After a few chuckles, they went outside and burned both lists in an old garbage can. As they watched them go up in smoke, they embraced each other for the first time in over a year. Later Brian and Ruth made a list of the *good* things that they admired about each other. Initially both lists were embarrassingly short, especially Brian's. But they kept adding to their lists as the days and weeks passed. Their respect and gratitude for each other grew deeper and deeper, truly enriching their relationship in countless ways. Every day is now 'Thanksgiving Day' for Brian and Ruth.

A spirit of gratitude and thanksgiving permeates a happy marriage. Both husband and wife make it a daily practice to thank God for their many blessings. This spirit of gratitude is a natural by-product of their genuine love and respect for each other. They learn lessons in perseverance during adversity, encouraging and supporting each other. They believe that nothing worthwhile in life, including a successful marriage, can be achieved without perseverance and commitment. It is an excellent idea for any couple to revitalize their marriage by periodically adding spice and variety to the daily routine. A complete change in daily routines and environmental surroundings is highly effective. The occasional weekend retreat is conducive to being caught up in the wonders of nature and God's creation. The commonplace can become wondrous and the wondrous can become commonplace when a happy couple walk hand-in-hand through an unspoiled forest with its wildlife, streams and lakes. The captivation of the imagination is surpassed only by the tranquility of the soul.

Every truly happy marriage has a spiritual foundation and relationship. Happy marriages do not 'just happen,' they are 'made;' this means that both husband and wife daily strive to build and maintain a serene loving atmosphere in the home. Their basic goals, values and priorities in life complement and blend with each other rather than conflict. Both accept the basic premise that marriage is an equal partnership in love in which each spouse shares rewards and adversities alike. The successful partners in a marriage practice the wisdom of openly sharing and discussing their problems, while never remaining angry or unforgiving. Mutual loyalty and respect are priceless treasures that both partners guard and preserve. They make a conscious effort to surround themselves with friends who share their spiritual faith, ideals and Christian principles.

Chapter V
Perceptions on Family

Love is the bond that holds every happy family together. Love flourishes in a home where all members of the family have an affectionate concern for one another. The most moving description of love in the whole Bible is found in Chapter 13 of 1 Corinthians, which is a penetrating summary of the character of Jesus. The central teaching of the New Testament proclaims that love is at the heart of the universe (John 3:16) and the most important commandment (John 15:12). The life and teachings of Jesus as recorded in the four Gospels are the manifestations of God's love. The invisible thread of God's love daily weaves the fabric that produces a close-knit family.

A five-year-old boy became confused and unsettled by the frequent bickering of his parents. One evening, following a lengthy quarrel with heated words exchanged between his parents, the youngster asked at the dinner table, "What do people say to each other when they get married?" His parents looked at each other somewhat embarrassed and bewildered by the question, waiting for the other to say something. Finally his mother said, "Why — they promise to love and be kind to each other." The young boy seemed perplexed by his mother's reply and said, "You and Dad aren't married a lot of the time, are you, Mom?" The sincerity of their son's words had a devastating impact on both parents. The father stared at his son, then glanced at his wife who reached over and took his hand as tears rolled down their cheeks. A few moments later, the father broke the hushed silence by suggesting something that had never been a custom in their home. He quietly asked that all heads be bowed while he said a prayer. Words did not come easily as he thanked God for the many blessings that he had been taking for granted. This was the beginning of a new *Spirit* in the home — Christ's Spirit of love and gratitude.

A happy family needs a happy marriage. A young mother had been quarreling frequently with her husband which had an unsettling effect on their marriage. One morning while taking a stroll on the beach with her mother, the daughter said, "Mom, I'm afraid of losing Jim; how does a woman hold onto a good husband?" Her mother thought intently, then without uttering a word, bent down and cupped up two handfuls of sand. As she slowly squeezed her left hand, the sand began escaping through her fingers; the harder she squeezed, the more sand disappeared. Then she gently held out her cupped right hand still full of sand. Her daughter gazed perceptively in silence and finally murmured, "I understand, thanks Mom." Without speaking a word, her mother dramatically taught a fundamental truth of human nature: *'Too tight a grasp stifles love.'* This silent lesson in human nature made the daughter realize that she was too possessive and self-centered in her relationship with her husband. With God's help she resolved to become more thoughtful and considerate which soon was reflected in her marital relationship.

Young couples who truly love their children appreciate the responsibilities as well as the rewards of raising a family. They realize that unsupervised and undisciplined young children can become helpless pawns and permanent losers. Parents who truly love their children do not give priority to affluent lifestyles over the basic needs of their children. They know that abdication of parental responsibilities in the crucial formative years shortchanges children for all time.

The teachings of the Bible are life's values for Livingwise Livingwell which should be woven deeply into the fabric of a child's upbringing. Parents should pass along to their children basic Biblical truths, the most fundamental being that no one is beyond the love or helping hand of our Creator. Basic truths and values are caught more than they are taught — parents should lead rather than merely point the way. This is in sharp contrast to attempting to instill a moral code of conduct that is seldom practiced by the parents. The only things of real value that parents can give their children are through daily example and a loving home environment.

Parents pass on their values to their children by how they live their daily lives. Their words, attitudes and even routine decisions reflect how they think and what is important. Moral and ethical behavior is prompted by the conscience which should be kindled early in life. This inner voice of conscience is a personal unwritten code which shapes character. A sense of values needs to be caught in the home where the character of children is shaped from the time they leave their mothers' womb. The young generation of today is presented with a confusing array of values, role models and interpretations. Words like 'love,' 'rights' and 'freedom' have lost their noble meaning as a result of widely varying moral and ethical standards in our secular society. Love without thoughtfulness withers with neglect; rights without responsibilities weaken character; freedom without accountability invites trouble.

The Bible repeatedly and consistently stresses parental responsibility in molding the character of their children. Throughout Scripture, the Bible depicts the father as teacher and guardian of spiritual values. The book of Proverbs is essentially an instruction manual written by a wise father to his children. He was one who loved his children (Genesis 37:4), but sometimes had to discipline them (Proverbs 3:12). He also instructed them (Proverbs 1:8), guided them (Jeremiah 3:4), exhorted and comforted them (1 Thessalonians 2:11), and strived to give them a proper upbringing (Ephesians 6:4). The wise father also controlled his children (1 Timothy 3:12), provided for their needs (2 Corinthians 12:14), and grieved over their folly (Proverbs 17:25).

Every personal experience can be a lesson in LIVINGWISE LIVINGWELL — a lesson of character in every adverse experience and a lesson of humility in every good fortune. Jesus' parable of the prodigal son (Luke 15:11-31) is a sterling lesson in genuine love, mercy and forgiveness. The younger of two sons became impatient and restless, unwilling to wait until his father's death to receive his inheritance. Far fields looked greener to him as he dreamed of 'sowing his wild oats and later praying for a crop failure.' After he had received and then squandered his inheritance, he returned home to ask his father's mercy and forgiveness. But his older brother became angry and resentful that his father welcomed his prodigal son with open arms. The true love of God was revealed in the father's words to his older son: "My son, everything I have is yours. But we must celebrate and rejoice, because this brother of yours was dead and is alive again; he was lost and is found."

Too many women delay marriage and forsake child-raising in deference to 'doing their own thing' or climbing the corporate ladder. Most of these advantaged women would be worthy mothers but choose well-paid careers, swelling the ranks of already overcrowded professions. Our affluent society has too many lawyers and financial advisers but too few dedicated mothers, teachers and nurses. Bearing children is not only a privilege but a great responsibility. Countless unloved children however are brought into this world by irresponsible or disadvantaged women. God never intended that countless thousands of 'crack' babies would be born — retarded, low IQs and prone to violent/criminal behavior when they reach adolescence. Nor does God intend that many more countless babies will never know a father or a loving home environment. Infants are taught and their character is shaped from the time they are born. In this life every infant may not get an *equal* chance, but every infant should be given a *fair* chance.

The withering away of the meaningful family is reflected in many facets of our society. Institutionalized day-care centers are a poor substitute for the early bond of mother and child particularly during the first three most formative years. Private home care, when necessary, is preferable to large day-care centers which are noted for low wages, inferior training of staff and high turnover of personnel. Where a financial burden exists, tax credits or subsidies should be available to enable the mother to stay at home. Nurturing a baby is not only gratifying to the devoted mother but necessary for the full development of the child. Stay-at-home mothers may be in the minority but they are willing to make temporary material sacrifices and delay business careers for the good of their children. Unfortunately, modern society has created the image of stay-at-home mothers as living in a cage — unfulfilled, with no identity or status, who can be liberated by a paycheck. Many women do great things, but a wife and mother of noble character surpasses them all. (Proverbs 31:29).

The traditional family structure has taken on the values of our permissive society. Single-parent homes, marital breakdown and divorce have become the norm rather than the exception. A generation of children is being raised who are afraid to love. They are developing a negative view of marriage which pushes them into insecure situations as they look for intimacy without love. The disintegration of the traditional family is magnified by the drug problem which in turn breeds crime and corruption. In a healthy family environment, the father is the spiritual leader while the mother responds to the needs of the children. Economic necessity may force some mothers to work outside the home but dollar bills can never bring back neglected formative years of childhood.

Many parents struggle selfishly for greater worldly 'success' at their children's expense. The popular concept of success captivates the secular mind, blinding many parents to their prime responsibility of molding the character of their children. Parental pursuit of the veneer of worldly success often leads to a hectic family life, taking its toll as children are turned over to day-care centers, babysitters and television. Many parents find that they are too busy, but in truth too indifferent, to devote adequate time to their children. Parental values and priorities become fuzzy without any knowledge of God's word, which makes it difficult to inspire authority and respect. A sense of strong moral and ethical direction is exerted when children are taught from a bedrock of truth. Parental guidance based on God's word has influence far beyond measure.

Solomon wisely perceived that 'the rich rule over the poor, and the borrower is servant to the lender' (Proverbs 22:7). The best way to learn how to avoid financial bondage is to follow a cash basis of financial management. Credit buying can create the illusion of prosperity, with small monthly installments and extended payment schedules. Countless families become caught up in the 'buy now, pay later' credit trap. They are under constant financial pressure simply because they are living a lifestyle beyond their means. Too much of their income is frittered away on nonessentials in an elusive attempt to achieve happiness. The key is to develop self-restraint and prudence in financial priorities, commitments and expenditures.

Credit is much like alcohol — if not used responsibly and in moderation, it can become an addiction. In business, the proper use of credit significantly facilitiates the flow of goods and services. On the personal level, mortgages are long-term, low-interest loans which enable young couples to purchase homes (which usually appreciate rather than depreciate in value). Living *with* credit is not the same as living *by* credit. Credit cards should be restricted to *one* for convenience purposes primarily while travelling (use plastic surgery on all other credit cards). The abuse of credit can become a financial curse when it results in financial bondage.

The place to start responsible management of money is to recognize that all family and personal expenses fall into one of two categories — wants or needs. A *need* is a biological necessity such as basic food, clothing and housing. A *want* is a desire of little urgency which is not set in motion by any basic necessity. In practice, credit should rarely, if ever, be used for *wants*. The practice of delaying purchases for *wants* until cash has been saved has a remarkably stabilizing effect on any family budget. Impulse buying becomes a thing of the past; by the time the needed cash is saved there is often a change of mind that the item is really wanted. Anticipation is often greater than the actual event of purchasing most *wanted* items. A sound practice is to avoid any new credit purchases on any *wanted* item until all current credit accounts have been paid in full. By practicing this kind of self-restraint, impulse buying is no longer a problem because savings are accumulated until *wants* can be bought for cash.

The family budget is a systematic method of living within the family income and minimizing extravagance. The only way to live within our means is to spend less than we earn. An effective budget gives priority to financial obligations over all other expenditures. Freedom from financial worry and stress, greater peace of mind, and increased harmony in the home emanate from responsible financial planning. Prudence, frugality and self-discipline are also cultivated which build character and self-esteem. In the following sample budget, monthly expenditures are shown as a percentage of total gross monthly income.

Summary of Financial Expenditures	% of Gross Income/Month
1. Tithe, 10% of net income (church, all other charitable organizations)	8
2. Savings	4
3. Income Taxes	16
4. Housing	21
5. Debts	2
6. Insurance (health, life, property)	5
7. Automobile (including depreciation)	10
8. Food	16
9. Clothing	7
10. Medical/Dental (not covered by insurance)	5
11. Entertainment (recreation, vacation)	4
12. Miscellaneous and unforeseen	2
TOTAL INCOME	100%

The savings habit can best be developed by setting family savings goals. Every payday we should *'pay'* ourselves first — deposit savings first, before spending the balance. Using direct deposit for automatic savings is painless as the decision to save is taken out of our hands.

A dollar saved is worth more than a dollar earned for three reasons — taxes are based on income not savings, most savings can be tax sheltered, and savings can be invested to earn interest. The 'Daily Compound Interest Rule of 72' states that 72 divided by the interest earned gives the number of years it takes for savings to double in value. For example, at six percent interest, savings double in twelve years; at nine percent, savings double in eight years; at twelve percent, savings double in just six years.

Four basic considerations should be taken into account in any savings investment — convenience, ease of converting to cash at any time, interest rate and degree of risk. A higher interest rate usually is associated with a higher risk. During periods of higher than normal interest rates, special effort should be made to invest extra savings in guaranteed certificates. Conversely, loans should be avoided if possible when interest rates are abnormally high.

The Christian home provides what human nature craves and needs the most — love, patience, understanding, forgiveness, acceptance and a sense of self-worth. It is in a Christian home environment where we learn to share and care and live together. The formative years in a child's life are the irrevocable years where he learns to relate to authority through loving parental discipline.

The prime responsibility of parents is to provide roots and wings for their children — roots of values and wings of self-reliance. Daily living provides ample opportunities for parents to practice moral values rather than merely preach them. Good parents are role models for their children to emulate; virtues such as common decency, patience, kindness and respect for others are imparted by parents in subtle words, tone of voice and little deeds. Parents should play a major role in molding and developing wholesome character in their children. Most delinquent children have delinquent parents; parental indifference or neglect rather than ignorance is the root cause of many heartaches. However, no parent is infallible or perfect; parents are human and need divine guidance in all areas of their lives including child-rearing.

Parental discipline that is expedient or inconsistent is usually initiated by emotional reaction. This kind of discipline undermines respect for the parent as well as the self-esteem of the child. Effective parental discipline relies on good communication and praise rather than punishment. The heart of the positive discipline approach is knowing how and when to praise the child — praise is not a substitute for rules which are essential. A continuing challenge for parents is deciding what is important and overlooking things that do not really matter. The long-term objective of parental discipline should be to teach children personal responsibility and accountability as they mature. During the adolescent stage gradual increase in responsibility and accountability builds self-esteem and decision-making skills, easing the teenager into responsible adulthood.

Children who are taught and encouraged to perform household duties generally lead more productive lives and become happier adults. They gain a sense of competence and self-esteem from feeling important and being useful members of the family. They understand the importance of cooperation and working together toward common goals. Children who regularly perform household tasks become more responsible, gain confidence and a feeling of self-worth which are key ingredients for emotional well-being.

The negative impact of excessive and indiscriminate viewing of television on children's lives is far reaching and incalculable. Some of the obvious effects in the classroom include shortened attention spans, insensitivity to violence and crime, passive attitudes toward learning and lack of respect for teacher's authority. Selective viewing of quality television programs is educational and beneficial but excessive or indiscriminate viewing can be harmful. During grade school, youngsters should be encouraged to read quality books that will take them back to the bookshelf rather than to the TV set.

Discipline accompanies all learning and wisdom. Parents are not only their children's first teachers but good parents are also their best teachers. As children reach the age of adolescence, they must possess the character and moral stamina to resist peer pressure and many temptations. They require an inner strength to wrestle successfully with life's complex problems and adversities. Wise parents guide their children in the various aspects of daily living so that they can manage the responsibilities and problems of adulthood.

The task of parenting will always be challenging but also rewarding. Childhood behavior is more than the result of parental influences — techniques that clearly succeed with one child can fail inexplicably with another. God has created us as unique individuals, capable of independent, rational thought that is not attributable to any source. In the early formative years of a child, parents should hold the reins of authority tightly. As the child approaches the difficult teenage years, parents must be prepared to loosen the reins gradually but systematically. Stormy episodes can be expected during adolescence which is characterized by conflicting desires to maintain the privileges of childhood while expecting the rights of adulthood. Teenagers are confronted by many temptations outside the home — drugs, alcohol, sex, obscenity, pornography, peer pressure.

There is no substitute for parental love based on Christian values. Love is demonstrated in all facets of parents' relationships with their children — tone of voice, patience, understanding, discipline. The graph on the following page shows the importance of Christian parental influence particularly during children's crucial formative years.

Proverbs 22:6 says, "Train a child in the way he should go, and when he is old he will not turn from it." This proverb implies that the offspring of wise and dedicated Christian parents will not stray from their godly training. The purpose of the book of Proverbs, written by Solomon who was the wisest man of his time, was to convey his divinely inspired observations of human nature and God's universe. The maxims in Proverbs uphold the law of *Cause* and *Effect* which states that '*a given set of circumstances can be expected to produce certain consequences.*' Proverbs are not absolutes but likelihoods whereby general truths are brought to

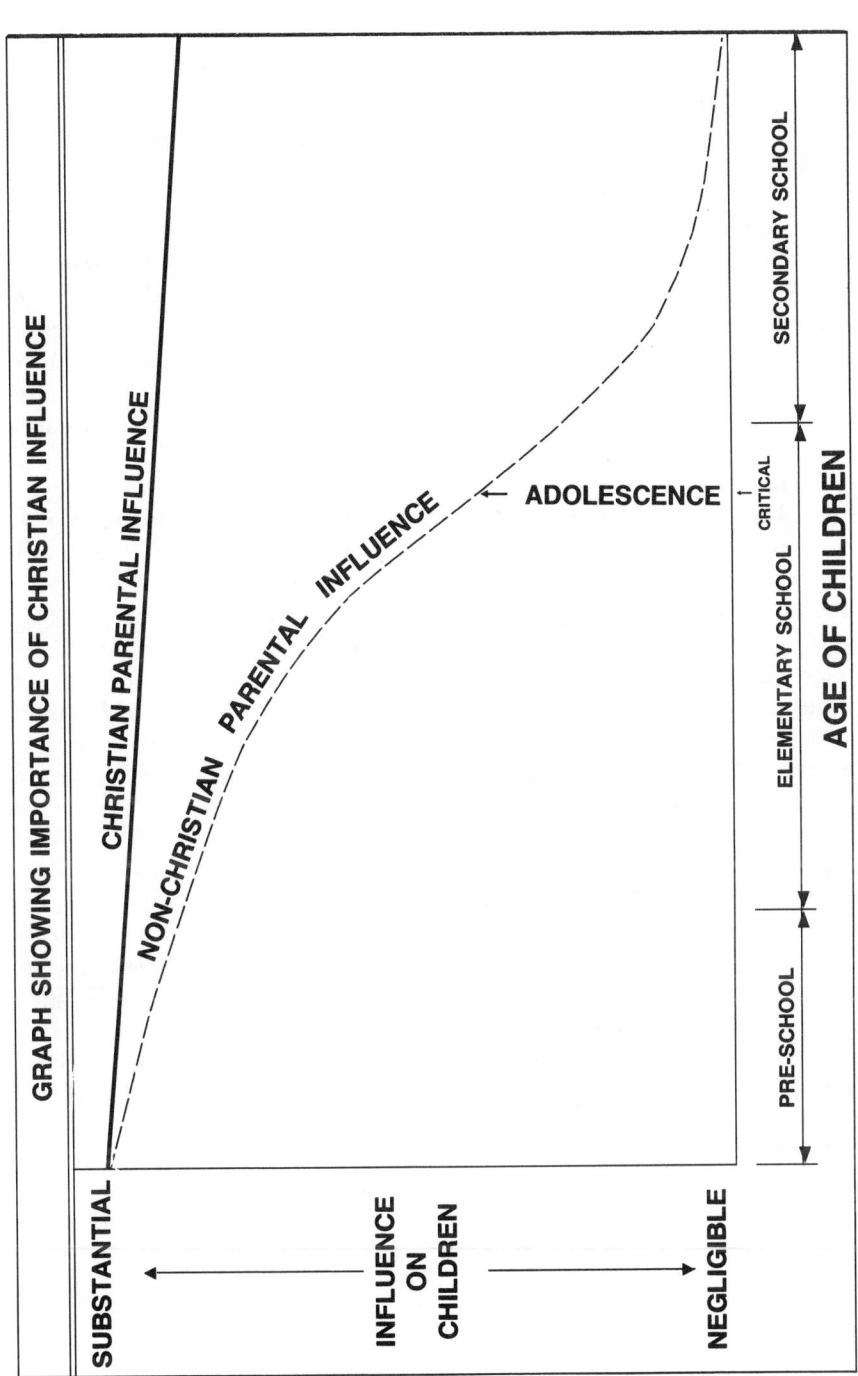

bear on specific situations. Proverbs are generally true but there is no ironclad guarantee or promise. Dedicated Christian parents who do their best to raise their sons and daughters properly can fully expect rich rewards even though there are no absolute guarantees.

A teenager met in private with the minister prior to formally becoming a church member. The minister praised the young man for being so faithful in attending Sunday School and asked him "What was it that I said that induced you to be a Christian?" Without hesitation the young man replied, "Nothing that I ever heard you say, sir, but rather the way my mother lived." This young man uttered words of profound truth. The mother, who by daily example teaches a child to love truth and purity, unconsciously sets in motion powerful influences that shape and transform his life a long as he lives. The child that is brought up in a truly Christian home has his life molded on a solid foundation of values and virtues that can never be undermined.

The early teenage years are crucial and the most challenging for parents. The parent/child must change to a parent/adolescent relationship. Adolescence is characterized by impatience for greater freedom without the burden of accountability. Mutual trust and respect are crucial; no one is perfect, not even parents or teenagers. Throughout the difficult adolescent period, the teenager should seek frequent counsel and advice from his parents, who in turn should be patient and understanding. As time progresses, the teenager gradually gains a greater measure of maturity and confidence in his decisions and actions. Responsible parents are ever-conscious that all too soon their fine teenager will sprout his wings and fly the coop.

Teenagers find it difficult to show love and respect for parents who are indifferent to their real needs. They have conflicting desires to hold on to certain privileges of childhood while at the same time expecting certain rights of adulthood. While outwardly rebelling against restrictions to their freedom, teenagers have insecurities and crave genuine parental guidance and counsel. They crave for greater freedom and independence but want and need parental patience and understanding. Loving parents want their teenage son or daughter to be acountable for their actions and decisions. This accountability, rather than the age of the teenagers, is the true measure of their maturity.

Parenthood is an endless series of small events, periodic conflicts and occasional crises. Every responsible parent wants their teenager to be guided by a core of values and a code of fairness. Good parents need skill as well as love to help their teenagers become independent adults. Wise parents make themselves increasingly dispensable as their teenagers mature. They sympathetically watch the drama of growth with some concern but allow their teenagers to make their own choices provided they are willing and able to live with the consequences. Teenagers crave independence but want their parents to be available for wise counsel. Teenagers are ready for adulthood when they can shoulder their own burdens, make decisions on their own and be willing to accept the consequences.

Unconditional love accepts others for what they are. Conditional love on the other hand often limits personal growth and fulfillment of those dearest to us. Parental conditional love can have near tragic consequences as demonstrated in the following story. Both parents were extremely proud of their only child, Julie. She was all that 'they' wanted her to be — including being near the top of her class every year. To her parents she was the ideal daughter, but Julie was masking a growing self-contempt as well as a seething resentment for her parents. They had built their own pedestal for her and Julie constantly struggled to reflect an approving image for them. She reluctantly played the role because she felt it was the admission price for her parents' love.

Finally Julie reached the breaking point and decided to end it all one evening by taking an overdose of sleeping pills. Desperately Julie struggled to the phone and dialed her girlfriend just before falling unconscious. Fortunately, medical assistance arrived in time and she fully recovered, but Julie couldn't go on masquerading. She told her parents how she longed to shed all the veneer and just be herself but she was afraid of losing their love. Julie went on to pour out her innermost thoughts and feelings. Tears rolled down their cheeks as her parents warmly embraced Julie and asked for forgiveness. They learned an unforgettable lesson — their daughter was a unique individual who wanted to be loved and accepted for what she was. They learned that genuine love must have no price tag or strings attached.

Chapter VI
Perceptions on Physical Health

Good health and physical fitness are by-products of a responsible lifestyle and should not be confused with diet fads, strenuous exercise or the like. Individuals who radiate good health and vitality take personal responsibility for their well-being. They demonstrate a wholesome zest for living and have a high resistance to disease. They minimize the risk of succumbing to heart attack, stroke, cancer and other serious diseases by avoiding harmful habits and following a responsible nourishing diet and exercise program. They live by the laws of cause and effect — as they sow, so do they reap the rewards of obeying the laws of healthy living.

The best things in life are free — above all else, good health and happiness. Prolonged poor health, however, is not conducive to happy living. Good health is a priceless treasure that we tend to take for granted — until we lose it. Good health cannot be bought at any price but it can be frittered away knowingly or unknowingly through ignorance, indifference or bad habits. Prolonged transgression of the laws of healthy living prepares the way for disease and serious illness. The old adage '*an ounce of prevention is worth a pound of cure*' applies to many areas of our lives, but none more vital than in matters relating to our health. Vigorous health does not happen by chance but is the result of obeying the laws of healthy living. When these laws are properly understood, good habits relating to our health become a way of life while habits which are injurious are shunned.

Human nature craves for the dramatic and sensational. Unfortunately however, there is nothing dramatic or sensational about preserving good health or preventing serious illness and disease. The media tend to be preoccupied with the curative aspects of sickness and disease as opposed to the preventive aspects. It is not easy to kindle a crusade for greater health awareness by young and old alike. But the wise teenage girl, who someday will marry and give birth, will not succumb to peer pressure or impulsive behavior which will inevitably bear bitter fruit. She realizes that dire consequences for the unborn child can result when the mother abuses or misuses her body through loose sex, alcohol, drugs, smoking or obesity. Responsible individuals adopt a lifestyle that reflects a simple truth — most of the causes of serious illness or disease are preventable through a wholesome lifestyle which produces an unusually high resistance to illness and disease.

The resilience of the human body is remarkable but it cannot be abused indefinitely without leaving some permanent scars. Nature is assisted in her effort to expel impurities and restore normal conditions in the body when unhealthy elements are removed and harmful habits are corrected. Common sense and good judgment are far more important than rigid rules, diet fads and extreme exercises. A nourishing balanced diet is the key ingredient for good health. The diet chosen for us by our Creator consisted of four basic food groups — grains, fruits, vegetables and fish. Simply and naturally prepared, these foods contain all the nutritive properties necessary for a balanced healthy diet. These primary foods are more wholesome than animal meat which is, in effect, secondhand food because the animal consumes primary foods for its own nutrition.

Cigarette smoking is a prime cause of coronary fatalities. Even moderate smokers have a much greater risk than nonsmokers of dying from a heart attack. While the use of low-tar/nicotine cigarettes may slightly decrease lung cancer risk, it has little or no effect in reducing the risk for cardiovascular disease. Smoking increases atherosclerosis in coronary arteries as well as in the aorta (the body's main blood vessel). Carbon monoxide displaces oxygen in red blood cells and nicotine constricts blood vessels (especially small ones). Cigarette smoke can also lower the threshold for ventricular fibrillation (an electrical instability of the heart muscle that can lead to sudden death). Fortunately, the risk of a heart attack and other diseases drops significantly within a few months of stopping cigarette smoking.

High blood pressure affects one in three of the adult population in North America. Yet only half are aware that they have hypertension, and less than a fifth are being treated effectively. Hypertension is the primary cause of stroke, a form of cardiovascular disease that blocks or ruptures the blood vessels that supply oxygen to the brain. Hypertension also contributes to many heart attacks. Any individual having blood pressure greater than 140 over 90 is hypertensive. The increased pressure exerted against the walls of the blood vessels can damage them. Excessive consumption of saturated fats and sodium in the diet along with excess weight contribute to hypertension. A responsible balanced diet and regular exercise (along with prescribed drugs as necessary when directed by physician) are effective treatments for lowering blood pressure.

There is broad agreement among medical experts that the risk of developing cancer or heart disease can be reduced significantly by *avoiding* or stopping cigarette smoking, *increasing* consumption of plant foods, and *decreasing* consumption of high-fat animal and dairy products. Most North Americans are suffering from a high-fat diet that lacks basic nutrition. Nutrition awareness rejects fad diets which disrupt the body's natural balance. *Not all calories are the same* — the energy from the fat calories cause overweight and other problems, but the energy from carbohydrate and protein calories are beneficial. Saturated fat raises blood cholesterol more than anything else in the diet. Saturated fat occurs in animal-meat products, whole milk dairy products and tropical vegetable oils.

Regardless of our chronological age, our physiological age is largely determined by the condition of our arteries. Healthy arteries are flexible and have smooth inner surfaces. The key to an *'artery-and-heart'* healthy diet is to minimize daily intake of cholesterol and saturated fats. Dietary fats are the most concentrated source of calories which is the prime cause of excess weight. Fat contains *more than twice* the calories in protein or carbohydrate. A further benefit in reducing the intake of saturated fats is that high blood cholesterol levels are lowered.

A healthy diet during childhood and adolescence is the best guarantee of good health during adulthood. Fat is the primary culprit that puts youngsters at risk in their adult years. Babies' growth-needs are exceptional for the first two years and fat intake offers a concentrated source of food energy. Beyond age two however, total fat should be restricted (no more than 30 percent of total calories of which saturated fat should be less than 10 percent). Fat intake, particularly *saturated* fat, should be restricted from the time children begin sitting at the table and eating adult food. For the young generation, healthy eating habits have to begin with the parents. They must know and practice healthy diets before they can teach and influence their children. *An ounce of prevention is worth more than a pound of cure years later!*

The human body needs only small amounts of cholesterol in the blood to function normally. Cholesterol is a soft waxy substance which is automatically manufactured by the liver in sufficient quantity. However, excess cholesterol is absorbed from consuming animal fat and certain dairy products. This excess cholesterol is carried in the blood through the arteries to all parts of the body. Cholesterol, like fat, does not mix with water. To carry both cholesterol and fat (lipid) in the blood, the body wraps them in protein-coated packages called 'lipoproteins.'

Our blood lipid profile gives a reliable indication of the condition of our arteries and the relative risk of coronary heart disease. Three measurements from a blood test make up our lipid profile — triglyceride level, high-density lipoprotein level, and low-density lipoprotein level. The triglyceride level measures fats in the blood. The high-density lipoproteins (HDL) contain a large amount of protein and a small amount of cholesterol. HDL are known as *'good'* lipoproteins because they take cholesterol away from the cells, transporting it back to the liver for excretion. High levels of good HDL are common in individuals who exercise regularly, do not smoke, and stay at normal weight. Dietary habits which lower fat and cholesterol consumption also tend to increase HDL levels which is a further beneficial effect.

The low-density lipoproteins (LDL) are largely composed of cholesterol. LDL are known as *'bad'* lipoproteins because high levels of LDL deposit cholesterol within the walls of the coronary arteries supplying blood to the heart. High triglyceride levels also result in fatty deposits circulating in the blood being deposited on the inner walls of the arteries. As more and more fat and cholesterol are deposited, the arteries become narrower and narrower. This process is called arteriosclerosis which is the most common form of heart disease. Over a period of years, this buildup of cholesterol and fat can seriously restrict blood flowing in one or more arteries to the heart. Ultimately an obstructing blood clot forms and the result is a heart attack. The risk of heart disease can be minimized by maintaining high HDL levels and low LDL and triglyceride levels in the blood.

The saturated fat content in the typical American diet is a prime contributor to high triglyceride and cholesterol levels in the blood. Saturated fat raises blood cholesterol more than anything else in the diet and should make up less than ten percent of our calorie intake. Solid at room temperature, saturated fat is found primarily in animal and dairy products. Three tropical oils often used in processing foods (palm, palm kernel, coconut) are also high in saturated fats. All oils contain three types of fat — saturated, polyunsaturated and monounsaturated. They are categorized by which type of fat predominates. Unsaturated fats are preferable to saturated fats, although all fats contain over twice as many calories as carbohydrates or proteins. Liquid at room temperature, unsaturated fats are found primarily in cooking oils, margarines and salad dressings. Monounsaturates lower the bad LDL and are therefore preferable to polyunsaturates which lower the good HDL in the blood.

A *'hit-list'* of high-fat foods to avoid include: certain dairy products (butter, cheese, ice cream), processed meat products, gravies, sauces, salad dressings, mayonnaise, fried foods, snack and junk foods. A wide variety of low-fat substitutes is readily available. Complex-carbohydrate low-fat foods (whole grain cereals and bread, potatoes, rice, pasta, corn, fruits) should be substituted for high-fat foods.

The single most important factor in lowering blood cholesterol is to consume less saturated fat. Cholesterol in the bloodstream comes from two sources — what the body manufactures (mainly by the liver), and what the body absorbs from food. There is much misleading advertising on food labels which is confusing to the consuming public. 'Cholesterol-free' labels on many food products are meaningless from a nutritional standpoint and misleading to the unwary consumer who does not read the fine print listing the ingredients. Deceptive advertising muddies the waters, selling the *image* but not the *fact* of good nutrition. Foods labeled *'cholesterol-free'* may be loaded with saturated fat which can elevate blood cholesterol levels much more than low-cholesterol foods having no saturated-fat content. Other foods labeled 'low-fat' or practically 'fat-free' usually refer to percentage by *'weight'* rather than by *'calories'* (which is the important factor). For example, a package of sausages may be labeled '95% fat-free' by *weight*, yet may be '50% fat' in *calorie* content.

Many individuals equate a healthy diet with a life of deprivation and self-denial. Fortunately it is possible to dramatically reduce consumption of harmful fats and cholesterol without undue sacrifice of enjoyment of food. Identifying high-fat foods and replacing them with lower-fat alternatives is far easier than counting calories or grams of fat. For example, *'lean'* ground beef has three times the fat of roasted chicken with the skin removed. Removing the skin from poultry cuts the amount of fat in half. Roasted turkey has even less fat than roasted chicken, while most fish (particularly flounder, sole and water-packed tuna) is the lowest in saturated fats of all meats. Switching to non-fat or low-fat dairy products is also an easy and painless way to reduce saturated fat intake (whole milk dairy products will soon taste like whipping cream). As we gradually change our diet, our tastes will also change with many *no-no* tempting foods losing their appeal.

The body uses up (or wastes) calories during the process of converting food into energy. This thermic effect is more pronounced for some foods than others. For example, the body burns about 25 percent more calories to get energy out of carbohydrates compared with fat. Since the body converts very little carbohydrates to body fat, a high-carbohydrate diet (whole-grain cereals, vegetables, fruit) is effective is losing weight, in addition to being wholesome and nutritious.

Carbohydrate foods are generally low in fat and contain no cholesterol. Carbohydrates contribute less than half the calories as do fats (four versus nine calories per gram). High-carbohydrate foods are also good sources of dietary fiber. Fiber is the nondigestible calorie-free part of plant foods that is highly beneficial in maintaining good health. High-carbohydrate, high-fiber, low-calorie foods include whole grain cereals, rice, raw fruits and most vegetables (particularly beans and potatoes). About 60 percent of our daily calories should come from carbohydrate food, 30 percent from protein, and 10 percent unsaturated fat.

Excessive consumption of salt is a major cause of high blood pressure. Salt is composed of sodium chloride, and sodium is the culprit. Excess consumption of sodium retains surplus water in the body causing tissues to expand, squeezing blood vessels thus increasing blood pressure. Common table salt and commercially prepared foods are the major sources of sodium in the North American diet. Products that list salt or sodium-containing additives near the top of the ingredients' list should be avoided. Salt shakers should also be removed from the table, and little or no salt used in cooking. Salt substitutes may be used for taste. The average North American diet contains about sixty times the amount of sodium needed by the body.

What we eat, how it is prepared, and how much we eat are all important factors in a wholesome diet. High-calorie salad dressings, butter and sauces should be minimized or avoided altogether and low-calorie substitutes used in moderation. Ample amounts of fiber-rich, unrefined foods have a space-filling effect and have relatively few calories while fresh fruit can be a tasty low-calorie dessert. All foods should be chewed slowly, savoring every mouthful. If time does not permit leisurely eating, it is preferable to skip a meal rather than gulp it down. Drinking one or two glasses of water one-half hour before a meal makes it easier to eat less, aids digestion, benefits the kidneys and contributes to intestinal regularity.

Water is the perfect beverage, having no calories, requiring no digestion and is exactly what the body needs for healthy functioning. Water is the most important substance we consume and is the largest single component of the human body (an average of 60 percent of body weight is water). Few of us realize the importance of water to the human body and consequently fail to drink enough of it. The average individual should drink *eight* glasses of water daily, preferably between rather than with meals; drinking water during meals dilutes digestive juices which retards digestion of food and can result in gas. Thirst is a signal that the body needs water replacement but it is not a reliable measurement of how much the body needs. Water carries waste products away from body organs, releasing toxins from the kidneys as urine and also through the skin as perspiration. The kidneys perform better in eliminating toxins with an optimal supply of water (keeps the urine pale). Adequate water consumption can also relieve constipation and alleviate dry, itchy skin. All of us can discover for ourselves the many benefits and higher level of well-being that can be ours simply by increasing our daily consumption of water.

Total caloric intake is the bottom line in reducing and controlling weight — in one week, 3,500 excess calories add one pound, but 3,500 fewer calories result in losing one pound. The food that we consume is potential energy and the body must burn up all this energy or store any excess calories as fat. However, what we eat is even more important than how much we eat for optimum health. Not only should saturated fats be avoided to maintain weight control and minimize risks of heart disease, but certain high-fat foods *increase* the risk of cancer. Excess consumption of high-fat animal meats and dairy products increases the risk of colon, breast and prostate cancer; also salt-cured, smoked and charcoal broiled meat can increase the risk of stomach cancer. On the other hand, regular consumption of high-fiber, whole-grain cereals, fresh vegetables and fruit reduce the risks of several types of cancer.

The body maintains what the mind harbors. At age 65, Noel Johnson was a physical wreck — his obese frame carried 95 excess pounds and he verged on being an alcoholic. He was considered too high a risk to retain life insurance coverage. His plans for retirement were shattered several years earlier when his wife died after a series of strokes. Noel was left with no real purpose or direction in his life. He spent most of his time watching television, drinking, smoking, getting fat and doing nothing constructive. His well-meaning son, wanting his father to have special care in his sunset years, suggested that he go to a nursing home. This remark jolted Noel and made him bristle! He decided then and there that it was high time to get control of his life. The next day he went to a jogging track and found that he couldn't jog even 100 feet. Eighteen years later, Noel Johnson had several senior records for distance running. The change in his life was nothing short of miraculous. He became a new man with a new lifestyle and a new commitment to life. Aside from his daily exercise program, he made major changes in his diet. He replaced his old staples of hamburgers, french fries and rich desserts with fresh fruit, vegetables, whole grain cereal/bread and low-fat milk. Noel Johnson is living proof that regardless of age our lifestyle really makes a difference to our health.

Permanent weight loss should be the main goal in any weight control program. This is in sharp contrast to the ups and downs of yo-yo dieting that can lead to various health problems as well as discouragement. Most fad diets work only temporarily because the body can tolerate an unbalanced diet for just a limited period of time. For this reason many crash weight-loss programs are harmful — any excess usually is its own undoing. The best weight-loss program includes regular aerobic exercise along with a nourishing balanced diet. Regular aerobic exercise results in losing fat and developing muscle, with less chance of regaining weight.

The best program should focus on sensible changes in nutrition and lifestyle. A low-fat, high complex-carbohydrate diet along with regular aerobic exercise is the best approach. It is never too late, even for yo-yo dieters, to regain control of their weight — all it takes is a little self-discipline and patience to reap the many rewards including improved health and a greater sense of self-worth. Everyone is human and fallible — the occasional departure or lapse should never be turned into a collapse or catastrophe by reverting to former unhealthy habits.

Health is a complete state of well-being, while fitness is a measure of how much blood the body can pump and how much oxygen it can process. Keeping fit not only results in having more energy and zest, but makes us feel good about ourselves. Any regular physical activity or moderate exercise that expends from 2,000 to 3,500 calories per week is highly beneficial. The health benefits of regular aerobic exercise go far beyond weight control — reduce risk of heart attack, lower blood pressure, lower cholesterol and triglyceride levels in the blood, and calming effect in overcoming stress.

The use of the Body Mass Index (BMI) rather than traditional height-weight charts is gaining acceptance in many countries. It is recommended as the most appropriate measuring technique and helps in setting up guidelines for prevention and treatment programs for weight problems. The BMI recognizes that there is a range of desirable weights for good health.

Perceptions on Physical Health

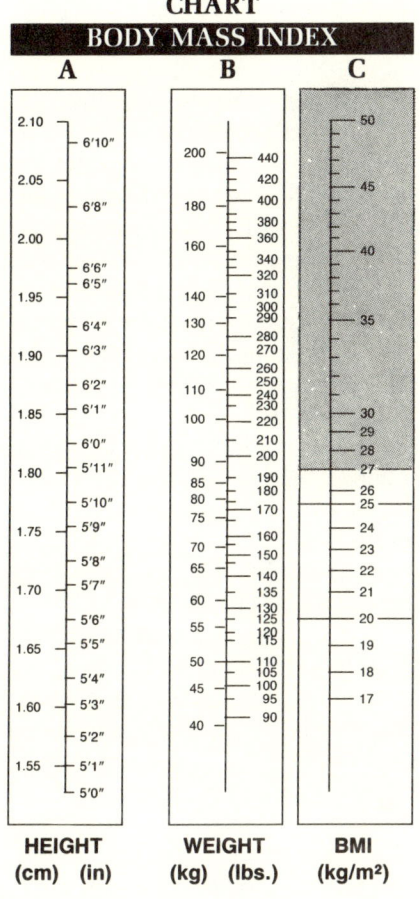

**CHART
BODY MASS INDEX**

Underweight (Under 20). A BMI under 20 may be associated with health problems for some individuals. It may be a good idea to consult a dietitian and physician for advice.

Normal Weight Range (20-25). This zone is associated with the lowest risk for most people. This is the range you want to stay in.

Slightly Overweight (25-27). A BMI over 25 may be associated with health problems for some people. Caution is suggested if your BMI is in this zone.

Definitely Overweight (Over 27). A BMI over 27 is associated with increased risk of health problems such as heart disease, high blood pressure and diabetes. It may be a good idea to consult a dietitian and physician for advice, especially if BMI is 30 or more.

How to find your BMI

1. Mark an X at your height on line A.
2. Mark an X at your weight on line B.
3. Take a ruler and join the two X's.
4. To find your BMI, extend the line to line C.

NOTE: The BMI works for adults between 20 and 65 years old. It is not accurate with children, adolescents, pregnant women or people over the age of 65.

Note: Above chart is based on following formula:

$$BMI = \frac{W}{2.2} \times \left[\frac{100}{H \times 2.54}\right]^2 \quad W = \text{weight in lbs.} \quad H = \text{height in inches.}$$

In any weight-loss program, we lose fat last where we put it on first — in the abdominal area for most men, and thighs and buttocks for most women. Fat cannot be turned into muscle, nor can muscle turn into fat. We need to lose fat and develop muscle. Aerobic exercise involving slow, steady-pace activity is safer and preferable to short bursts of exhaustive exercise for conditioning the heart and burning off calories. A small amount of regular exercise goes a long way toward preventing heart disease. The beneficial effect of physical fitness is substantial, especially for individuals with risk factors such as high cholesterol and blood pressure.

There is a close relationship between lifestyle and health. One important aspect of a healthy lifestyle is suitable, regular exercise — it is not only vital to overall good health but it enables the body to maintain a reserve that has a protective effect during times of stress. However, good judgment and common sense need to be used especially in the early stages of any exercise program. Too much or too strenuous exercise not only invites injury but can weaken rather than strengthen immunity to illness and disease. The time spent in daily aerobic exercise is more important than the distance covered — for example, an overweight individual loses one pound a month with a 20-minute daily walk but four pounds a month with an hour-walk each day.

Walking is much safer than running — the risk of injuries such as torn tendons, sprains and bone fractures is much greater while running. Walking is also just as beneficial. For an individual of average build, walking at a slow-to-moderate pace of 3 miles per hour burns 64 calories per mile, while brisk walking at 5 miles per hour burns 128 calories per mile. This compares to the average jogger who burns 100 calories per mile. Brisk walking is not only safer than running, it also burns more calories per mile. Bike cycling (either indoor or regular outdoor) is a good alternative when walking is not practical or suitable. Swimming is also a good alternative — it is virtually injury-free because it is a non-weight bearing activitiy (swimming ¼ mile burns 300 calories).

Walking is the safest type of exercise regardless of age. It is the oldest and most natural exercise and should be part of a daily routine. One delightful benefit of a brisk walking program is that we can lose weight without eating less. It is an excellent, safe method to shed excess pounds and keep our weight under control. Weight loss from regular walking is safe, gradual and natural, unlike crash dieting. The muscles of our legs, hips, stomach, chest and shoulders are all involved in brisk walking. A brisk steady pace for 45 minutes daily will also benefit the lungs, heart and complete circulatory system. However, walking should gradually increase in pace until a brisk pace can be maintained (train, don't strain). Any walking program should begin with a moderate pace for several days, gradually increasing to the level of a brisk walk.

Walking is helpful in preserving emotional health. It has a calming, tranquilizing effect and provides therapeutic relief from stress-producing concerns like tension, anxiety, depression and insomnia. It is very difficult to remain angry, irritable, tense or upset during or following a long walk especially in attractive surroundings. In addition, the mere passage of time while walking gives us the opportunity to obtain a better perspective on whatever may be troubling us. It sharpens our senses and enhances our concentration and creative powers. After several weeks of daily walks, the body develops more stamina and is less susceptible to fatigue.

A retired physician related the story of two middle-aged business executives who had similar coronary by-pass operations on the same day. Both operations were a complete success and their progress following surgery was excellent. Both were discharged from the hospital on the same day yet one man changed little and before long he resumed his former lifestyle along with his bad habits. He ignored medical and family advice to discontinue several harmful habits. Nine months after his operation he had a fatal heart attack. However, the other man did some serious thinking and soul-searching following his discharge from the hospital. He learned some valuable lessons which altered his basic values and priorities. His family and friends were now at the center of his life rather than on its periphery. People became more important than things. He gave up several bad habits which were injurious to his health, followed a low-fat balanced diet and enjoyed a daily 3-mile walk before breakfast. Nine years after his operation, he is healthier and happier than before his bypass surgery.

Chapter VII
Perceptions on Mental Health

Whatever is true, whatever is noble, whatever is right, whatever is pure, whatever is lovely, whatever is admirable — think about such things (Phil. 4:8). Those things which occupy our mind most of the time determine what kind of individuals we become. Like pollution of the environment, pollution of the mind is an ever-present by-product of our permissive society. Our mental diet requires self-discipline in the same way as our physical diet. By exercising mental self-discipline we can cultivate wholesome, healthy thoughts and a positive outlook on life.

Through determined effort we can alter the current of our thought-patterns by fixing the mind upon positive things. As we cultivate a spirit of gratitude, we become more appreciative of the many benefits and blessings which God has strewn in our pathway. Our thoughts and our beliefs shape our attitudes which are reinforced and nourished as we give them utterance.

The mind is much more than the working of the human brain. The influences of the mind acting on the brain results in human will. Our state of mind affects how we perceive the world around us and how we think and act. Our mental attitude has an impact on the choices we make and the values we choose to live by; these in turn are closely linked to our general well-being.

The human mind is a powerful weapon against disease. Many individuals overcome serious disease and illness simply because they refuse to give in. They possess the belief and will to overcome their illness, and this positive spirit prompts changes in their body chemistry and strengthens their immune system. The human body responds to positive thoughts and strong convictions by fostering conditions that contribute to good health and general well-being.

Medical research has identified specific links between the mind, the brain and the immune system. There is solid evidence that the brain and immune system communicate through a family of hormones and other elements in the blood. The immune system is a complex, alert defense network which shields the body against viruses and bacteria. None of our bodily systems is more important than the immune system in protecting our physical well-being. Prolonged mental stress, anxiety or depression can play havoc with the immune system, but a positive mental attitude and hopeful outlook on life help the immune system function normally and effectively.

Occasional emotional stress is normal but constant stress suppresses the immune system, leaving the body vulnerable to disease and illness. Emotional stress is the body's response to any demand which is placed on it. Individuals under constant stress eventually feel overwhelmed, unable to cope or feel in full control of their lives. The human body cannot tell the difference between situations that are actually life-threatening and those that are present in thought only. The mind can spin out endless fantasies of possible disasters when negative thoughts of gloom are allowed to dominate. As we think, so are we; as we continue to think, so we become. A cheerful heart is good medicine (Prov. 17:22) and a heart at peace gives life to the body (Prov. 14:30).

The area of greatest importance to real happiness and peace of mind is choosing and controlling our thoughts. Cultivating the mental discipline to practice positive thinking strengthens the fabric of our daily lives. Cheerfulness, inner joy and peace of mind are contagious and cannot be hidden. Certain individuals stand out from the crowds of passers-by, their faces emanating a glow of deep contentment and love. Other individuals choose to live in their gloomy thoughts, carrying around in their minds tape recordings of unpleasant memories from the past and worries about the future. These mental tapes form deep grooves in the subconscious mind that are not easily erased.

Moods are governed by how our minds interpret experiences and what our expectations are for the future. It is important to perceive that unless we manage our moods, our moods will manage us. Once we accept personal responsibility for controlling our moods, we can automatically begin cultivating a more positive attitude and outlook on life. An attitude is the state of mind with which we approach situations in our daily living. One day we could have a positive upbeat attitude, while another day we could have a negative attitude toward our problems or even life in general. On both days the only difference is our *attitude* which only *we* can control. Our attitude affects what we do, what we say, how we behave and even how we feel and speak. Our attitude or state of mind affects every area of our personal lives and is crucial to our general wellbeing and happiness.

Chronic complaining and a pessimistic outlook on life reflect a spirit of ingratitude. Minor irritations which should be taken in stride trigger strong reactions. By contrast, a spirit of gratitude can make all the difference in having a cheerful disposition and optimistic outlook on life. Norm and George, two business associates I knew, illustrate this contrast. Norm is very fortunate indeed, much more in fact than most people. He is blessed with good health, has a university education, a lovely wife and two children, and good position in an established company. But Norm is never happy, seldom smiles and always seems to look on the dark side of things. When anyone says "Good morning, Norm" even on a bright, sunny day, he invariably replies, "What's good about it?" Norm just naturally gripes about everything and never seems to have a good word for anyone or anything.

On the other hand, George has a cheerful disposition and goes out of his way to brighten the lives of others. Outwardly he has little to be thankful for — chronic health problems, little formal education, a handicapped wife and menial type of job. But George never complains about his problems or his lot in life simply because he possesses a genuine spirit of gratitude. His heart literally throbs with God's love. His cheerful disposition and optimisitc outlook on life lift the spirits of all who are fortunate enough to know him.

The inherent power of the human mind can be constructive or destructive. Habitual negative thought-patterns magnify problems and can become a powerful 'trojan horse' which undermines a healthy body, mind and spirit. But the sheer force of positive thought is all-powerful in overcoming negative thinking. Within everyone lies an irresistible divine urge to experience the fullness of life at its best. The more that we consciously allow good, true and wholesome thoughts to dwell in our consciousness, the more certain it becomes that we become a magnet for attracting goodness into our lives. We can literally change our lives by merely changing our thinking — positive thought is the father of all noble endeavors, setting unseen forces in motion that bring positive results. As we think, so we are; as we continue to think, so we become.

The average person is more likely to be 'nibbled to death' by the accumulation of everyday irritations and hassles than to be suddenly overwhelmed by some personal tragedy. Daily irritations can trigger bad moods in some individuals while others take hassles in stride. Problems are challenges and character-builders for some individuals but obstacles and frustrations for others. Missing a train or being delayed by traffic snarls can be very stressful to one individual but only a minor inconvenience to another. The difference is how the two individuals respond.

Maintaining a proper perspective when unexpected problems arise is important in controlling negative reactions. Individuals who feel in control of their lives and view problems as challenges are better able to handle stressful situations and routine hassles. We can add years to our life and life to our years by learning to master our responses to stress.

Worry, tension and anxiety are the most common maladies in our modern society, yet there is no medical cure. Worry is an irrational state of mind that harbors unhealthy thoughts. It is the most universal of all bad habits, as it diminishes the quality of life and does not contribute in any way to resolving personal problems. Worry begins with a trickle of negative thinking but can become a self-destructive habit over a prolonged period of time, channeling a deep groove in the subconscious mind that is difficult to erase.

The best way to overcome worrisome thoughts is to swamp them with more powerful positive thoughts of faith, hope and love. Rather than becoming victims of destructive unhealthy thoughts, we can become masters of our own minds by choosing constructive, productive thought-patterns. The power of positive thinking is such that it can erase anything not in harmony with itself.

Depression has been called the "common cold of mental disorders." All of us experience disappointments in life that cause some mild depression which usually runs a normal course and dissipates within a few hours or days at the most. However most of us, sooner or later, will experience a few instances of extreme depression during our life. This gut-wrenching type of depression makes the heart ache as the mind reruns the tragic events and circumstances in gruesome detail until they become all-consuming and all-encompassing.

Prolonged depression leads to chronic anxiety which can have many adverse effects — becoming apathetic, listless, unresponsive, isolated. These direct effects can have widespread consequences — marital, family, social and business. Normally, the passage of time and support of loved ones help to get 'over the hump' as the victim begins to think more and more about the future rather than the past. However, sometimes depression does not run its normal course, and the victim develops a dismal outlook on life and becomes more and more isolated. In instances where severe depression lasts several weeks and does not ease with the passage of time, professional assistance is in order.

The 'black dog' of depression stalks countless individuals of all ages in all walks of life. The symptoms of depression can be purely psychological or a combination of mental and physical complaints. Genetically, some individuals are more susceptible to depressive moods than others; some traumatic experiences early in life can be echoed by psychological stress later in life.

Depressed moods come in many colors and degrees of severity, from the occasional blues to blackest despair. The boundary between normal gloomy moods and clinical depression requiring professional attention is not easy to identify. Short periods of discouragement and sadness are part of normal living, particularly after a major loss or physical illness. These depressed moods usually last a few days or weeks at the most, and usually do not interrupt the business of everyday life. Among the bereaved, depressed moods may be quite severe and last several months. The incidence of prolonged depression, however, is more prevalent among individuals with little faith in God and few social supports (family, friends, loved ones).

Persistent thoughts and feelings of disappointment, rejection and irritability are usually early signs of potential depression. Later signs include general apathy and withdrawal, and having a dismal outlook on life. Life ceases to have any zest, and interests which were formerly appealing become tedious. Negative thoughts of worthlessness and emptiness dominate the mind as feelings of inadequacy wear the depressed victim down to the point of despair and hopelessness. These feelings of low self-esteem and self-worth often lead to unhealthy dependencies on harmful substances.

Our thoughts and our attitudes are the fathers of our behavior, while our beliefs and convictions shape our values and priorities. The conscious and subconscious feelings which we have about ourselves form our self-image. Self-esteem is related to our inner self while self-confidence relates to our outer self. Self-confidence is task-oriented and is a feeling that we are capable of performing certain skills. On the other hand, self-esteem is a feeling that we are worthwhile and that our lives count for something. When we have a healthy self-esteem, we have a good feeling toward ourselves which makes it easy to show love for others. Happy individuals have a deep appreciation for the gift of life; they are tough-minded but tender-hearted, perceiving some positive meaning and significance even in adversity.

Lack of self-esteem and absence of a spirit of gratitude are the greatest barriers to personal happiness. Individuals who lack a feeling of self-worth and self-respect become self-centered and insecure. They lack faith in God, in themselves and in other people which produces cynicism. They demonstrate little interest or concern for others as they become victims of self-pity and self-centeredness. Left unchecked, low self-esteem can have an accumulative snowball effect. The result is invariably a pattern of irresponsible behavior reflected in self-destructive habits and bad decisions. Gradually their hearts can become hardened and their souls shriveled as they wither away spiritually, losing any appetite for the things of God.

Happy individuals feel comfortable with who they are and what they are. A basic element in their philosophy is having a sense of self-worth and self-esteem. They are able to let go of anger, resentment, jealousy and other unhealthy feelings. They have a genuine interest in people and have a way of making others feel comfortable and relaxed in their presence. They focus their thoughts and activities outside themselves where they find meaning and purpose in their lives. By contrast, individuals with a poor image of themselves are locked in a continuous self-awareness, ever conscious of shortcomings or inadequacies which are grossly magnified in their mind. Their poor self-image can be expressed in many ways — ranging from a constant effort to impress people in trivial ways to the other extreme of social withdrawal and depression.

It is an inspiration to know someone who possesses a rare 'touch of class,' a virtue that is easy to detect but difficult to define. Their quiet, self-confident manner bespeaks an aristocracy that has nothing to do with wealth or position. Others feel comfortable in their presence simply because they are comfortable with themselves. They usually have a rare sense of humor and know that an occasional good laugh is the best lubricant for oiling the machinery of human relations. They do not dwell on their mistakes or the mistakes of others. Knowing that life consists of a series of ups and downs, they take their misfortunes with grace and their successes with humility. Their genuine character leaves no room for any pretense or hypocrisy. Their 'touch of class' makes them stand out from the crowd as unique individuals.

Sooner or later, all of us experience personal crises — sorrow, suffering and grief are inevitable but some individuals experience more than their fair share. Although we are living in a death-denying society, the one unavoidable fact of life is death; in the midst of life all around us, death is ever-present. Each one of us has to do our own believing and ultimately our own dying. Death of a loved one is a deep wound, and the grieving process must run its course as it works to gradually heal the wound.

It is best to face grief head-on, taking one day at a time.

Grief over the loss of a loved one is a very lonely experience but it should never be denied. Grief has a logic all its own and getting through it takes time. Stifling the emotions of grief only delays the recovery process. The individual who has built a support system of close friends can best handle grief as God does his healing work through other people. The grieving individual, above everything else, needs the concern and caring of God's messengers of love.

The bereaved individual experiences powerful emotions that need to be released. The best first greeting is simply, "I'm sorry" and/or an appropriate note in a sympathy card. It is not necessary to have a dialogue, a conversation or even to respond to the grief-stricken. There is often a power and a beauty in a caring silence and presence that surpasses mere words. The power of the attentive ear is remarkable, especially during a time of grief. For the individual in a state of shock and grief, daily mundane tasks often seem irrelevant and difficult. The greatest comfort for a grieving individual is a deep personal faith in the immortal soul and life hereafter.

Loneliness is an unhappy state of mind that affects how we think and how we feel. Prolonged loneliness can become a chronic malady, feeding on self-pity, isolation from friends, and feelings of being unwanted or unneeded. Invariably loneliness reflects an absence of any meaningful involvement or sense of purpose. Being lonely, however, is not the same as being alone. A feeling of emptiness and loneliness can be experienced even in a large crowd, yet times of solitude can be most creative and peaceful.

Lack of any sense of purpose or meaningful involvement often leads to boredom — a vacuum in the human spirit that demands to be filled. Prolonged boredom can produce restlessness which may lead to unhealthy diversions (alcohol, gambling, overeating, etc.). Restlessness is a signal that should goad us out of complacency and stagnation, spurring us on to some lofty goal. The diligent pursuit of worthwhile goals satisfies the natural craving in all of us for a sense of self-worth and accomplishment.

When a personal injustice is allowed to become an obsession in our mind, resentment and bitterness begin to grow and fester. The memory becomes a videotape that plays reruns of old rendezvous with pain over and over again. Deep-seated anger turned inward leads to resentment, bitterness and self-pity which undermines positive feelings of self-worth. Injustices and misfortunes can make us either a *better* or *bitter* individual, the important difference being that one has 'i' in it.

Forgetting injustices or forgiving wrongs is not easy, especially when we feel the sharp pain of festering wounds. But recalling wrongs or carrying a grudge is wretched justice for not forgiving and forgetting. We can choose to drown ourselves in regret and cling to old injustices; that is our choice but not our destiny. In a spirit of forgiveness and gratitude, we can rise above lingering feelings of personal grievances and injustices, freeing ourselves from the poison of bitterness and resentment.

An illustration of a positive outlook on life that left an impact on me occurred one Saturday at a supermarket. It was crowded and many of the women were irritated and impatient with their children. Laden down with groceries in shopping carts, several mothers were taking their frustrations out on their children as they were leaving the supermarket. Then a mother, permanently handicapped and confined to a wheelchair, came out with her young son on her lap holding a bag of groceries. As she waited for her husband to arrive from the parking area in their old-model car, she gave the wheelchair a slow spin. Both mother and son laughed with glee; then she gave the chair another faster spin and they both laughed heartily and hugged each other. By this time her smiling husband had arrived and gave her a tender kiss as he lifted her from the wheelchair into the car. This handicapped mother was so richly blessed with the joy of living that she felt compelled to share it with her son. What she didn't know was that she also shared her joy with me, a total *stranger!*

There is much truth in the old adage, "Laugh and the world laughs with you, cry and you cry alone." A good sense of humor can be cultivated by looking for the funny side of things that can happen every day. One sign of a good sense of humor is to be able to chuckle at our own mistakes rather than those of others. We can use our sense of humor to cheer up someone who hasn't had much to laugh about. A good sense of humor not only helps cheer us up in handling everyday problems and frustrations, but it is also beneficial to our general health and well-being. A hearty laugh now and again is beneficial for our internal organs. Our facial muscles, thorax, diaphragm and abdomen simultaneously get invigorating exercise, followed by complete relaxation. But beyond the physical benefits, the psychological and spiritual advantages are also rewarding.

A smile costs nothing, but creates much. It cannot be bought, begged, borrowed or stolen. No one needs a smile more than someone who has no smile to give. A captivating smile comes from within, speaks louder than words, and is the shortest distance between two strangers. A smile takes only a moment but its memory can last forever.

Meditation is a key to a better understanding of our inner selves and the world around us. It allows us to delve to the very core of our being, enabling us to know more clearly our real needs as distinct from our evident wants. Meditation promotes general well-being, reduces stress and tension, and induces a calm, serene perspective on life. Meditation is most effective in a quiet, peaceful environment with no distractions.

A positive, trusting attitude along with a spirit of gratitude are very conducive to a serene state of mind. Peace of mind has little to do with the world around us but everything to do with what we inwardly feel and believe. Through meditation we can undress our mind of the things of this world and catch a fleeting vision of the eternal.

Meditation is directing our thoughts in the ways of God. Reflecting upon God is most effective when our thoughts are directed toward inspiring Biblical truths and earnest prayer. Regular meditation increases our awareness of God's presence and deepens our faith. Even minute "vacations" taken out from our busy schedules to meditate upon God can help untangle the threads of hectic living. These brief moments of meditation choke the seeds of worry, anxiety, anger and frustration as we seek to deal with the daily irritations of life. Meditation increases our perception and discernment of spiritual values and truths, and gradually weaves them into the fabric of our minds. Through meditation, our thoughts can assume a penetrating quality that enables us to discover deeper truths about God, His world and our place in it. Meditation brings us closer to God and makes us sensitive to the needs of others.

Prayer is an opportunity to explore a relationship with the infinite mystery of life. It can become a doorway through which we can discover new dimensions of our being. In sacred quiet moments, we can deepen our awareness of life's goodness and whisper to God in gratitude. There is something special about praying for the well-being of others and having others pray for us.

Negative thinking is the cause of most personal problems. Learning to erase thoughts of fear and doubt with thoughts of love and faith is the greatest adventure of the mind. The more that we contemplate those positive things that are desirable, the easier it becomes to overcome fear through faith. The only limits to the manifestation of the spirit within us is the limitations of our thoughts. By learning to think in absolute rather than relative terms, we can perceive the true nature of things rather than allow our mind to be shackled by the mere appearance of things. We cannot fully understand or perceive the seen without having faith in the unseen. By choosing to focus our thoughts on positive things we open our heart and mind to all the blessings of love and happiness.

Our thoughts and attitudes are like magnets, attracting or repelling good into our lives. We take charge of our lives by first taking charge of our thoughts. We are drawn toward those things which we mentally image. By taking charge of our mind, we become the stewards of our destiny. We should be conscious of the kinds of thoughts that move in and out of our mind, ignoring negative thoughts that do not contribute to our betterment and well-being.

As we consciously allow only good, true and healthy thoughts to enter our mind, we are in harmony with the power of God living in and through us. Love transforms fear into faith because God is love. True happiness comes from an inner awareness of our unity with a Divine Power infinitely greater than ourselves — the Author and Creator of every good and perfect gift.

It is natural to reminisce as we get older, recalling wonderful times in the past. Nostalgia can be most inviting because what really matters is not the way it was but the way we remember it. However, we should not sacrifice our enjoyment of the present by placing undue emphasis on what happened long ago. To truly experience and enjoy the moments of the present, we must be willing to let go of things which are no longer useful. The snares of unpleasant memories can become shutters to the mind, blocking the sunshine of today which can brighten every corner of our lives. Now is the time to treasure the gift of today, living each moment to the fullest, knowing that goodness and beauty are in the heart and mind of the beholder.

Happiness is a state of well-being and inner peace that comes from an awareness of the goodness of God. This awareness of the spirit of God within us and living through us emanates a calmness and authority founded on truth and goodness. Happy are those who have an abiding faith in a Higher Power and draw on this inner source of strength. Their faith is more powerful than their adversities, and their thoughts are directed to concern for others rather than themselves. They recognize that value and worth are divine endowments rather than human attainments, and that love is the essential ingredient for personal happiness.

The Bible tells us, "Happy are the pure in heart." The heart is the seat of our conscience, the center of our motives and the residence of our will. Man-made laws lack the essential element to purify human nature — the power to cleanse the heart of selfishness, envy and greed. Ignorance and greed contribute to vice and crime, but virtue does not issue forth from knowledge and education. Purity of heart does not come from mental resolve, environment or education, but rather through repentance and personal faith in God. Pure lives stem from pure hearts. Human nature has its inherent imperfections but the elusive qualities of character and personality set us apart.

The old adage *'The proof of the pudding is in the eating'* is never more evident than when we apply the timeless truths of God's word in our daily lives. The transformed Christian life is not abstract theology but affects how we think and choose to behave each day of our lives. When our faith is real, it is clearly evident in our behavior. Faith without deeds has little value because genuine faith inevitably produces good fruit. We become *'difference makers'* in an indifferent world when our growing faith brings out the best in us.

Our state of mind affects how we think and act. Our thoughts and our beliefs are reinforced and nourished as we give them utterance. Repeating the 23rd Psalm to ourselves has an excellent therapeutic, calming effect on the mind whenever something is troubling us. The benefits will be remarkable when we develop the habit of repeating this wonderful passage of Scripture. It will have a positive ripple effect on many areas of our lives, even on what we think, say and do.

Psalms 23

The Lord is my shepherd, I shall lack nothing.
   He makes me lie down in green pastures,
He leads me beside quiet waters,
   He restores my soul.
He guides me in paths of righteousness
   for His name's sake.
Even though I walk through the valley of
   the shadow of death,
I will fear no evil, for You are with me;
   Your rod and Your staff, they comfort me.
You prepare a table before me in the
   presence of my enemies.
You anoint my head with oil;
   my cup overflows.
Surely goodness and love will follow me
   all the days of my life,
and I will dwell in the house of the
   Lord forever.

Chapter VIII
Perceptions on Spiritual Health

Spiritual health and genuine happiness go hand-in-hand. The finite human mind can never fully grasp the infinite love and power of God. While belief has a certain degree of conviction based on intellect and rationalization, faith always embodies trust in the unseen. We cannot grow spiritually and remain the same. Whenever we take a voluntary step towards allowing God to move from the periphery to the center of our lives, we change and grow spiritually. Good works and deeds should never become a substitute for Christian faith but rather a natural by-product of a living faith. Lofty goals and ideals are inherent in a living faith, but there are no shortcuts to spiritual growth. There are no quick fixes, fast answers or easy solutions to the problems of this world as we write our personal Book of Life.

In our pilgrimage through life's uncharted waters, God alone is the divine answer to our deepest needs. The happiness that flows from goodness and truth in our lives has enduring worth even though our lifetime here on earth is merely a moment in eternity. Our future is as bright as the sovereign promises of God when we develop a close personal relationship with our Creator. Inner peace and joy are the rewards of spiritual growth as we earnestly seek to know God better through studying and meditating on His Word. The ultimate goal in spiritual growth should be to make every principle and truth in Scripture a reality in our daily lives.

God is the Creator and Author of all life, in Him we live and move and have our being. A whole new world can be opened to us when we become aware of the reality of His love which is at the heart of the universe. Life at its best can be much like a lovely flower that has all too brief a life span to bloom. We can marvel at the beauty and wonder of nature in which everything is unique yet keeps on changing — buds bursting in the spring, leaves falling in the autumn, morning glories opening at sunrise and closing at sunset, ocean tides imperceptibly rising and receding, everything gradually but surely changing. We can drink in the soft texture of a petal, the veined perfection of a leaf, the mournful call of a mother loon, or the soft sounds of a babbling brook. We have eyes to see and ears to hear, yet too often we are insensitive or indifferent to the common things in nature. We need to be more like the great artist who finds new ways of perceiving the ordinary, the familiar, the commonplace.

Within each one of us lies a divine urge to experience the fullness of life at its best. We need to perceive the good life as a matter of personal choice rather than as a game of chance. The area of greatest importance to spiritual health and well-being is choosing and controlling our thoughts. We can literally change our lives by merely changing our thinking — as we think, so are we; as we continue to think, so we become. Where our treasure is, there are hearts will be also; whatever is important to us captures our thinking. The more that we consciously allow loving and peaceful thoughts to dominate our mind, the more we will attract love and peace in our personal lives. A spirit of gratitude and love begins to flow, enabling us to rise above self-centered frustrations and grievances.

The seeds of greatness lie within each one of us, waiting and begging to be nourished. Lofty goals and ideals are inherent in a living faith which has a divinely inspired vision of the future. Great hopes are life-giving but feeble expectations are life-draining. Hope is a noble vision of the future that trusts in a Power greater than any problems. Perseverance and hope can overcome the moral chaos and confusion of our sinful world. The diligent pursuit of worthwhile goals satisfies a wholesome craving for personal fulfillment. To translate goals into realities, they must be held vividly on our 'mental screen' day-in and day-out. Living a life of expectancy and anticipation, the future is as bright as the sovereign promises of God.

Failure to live up to an ideal does not invalidate the ideal. Character building is the work of a lifetime, the struggle for conquest over self being a lifelong struggle. Beset with temptations large and small, we should never act from selfish impulse. In one brief moment, we can place ourselves in the power of evil through some hasty, unguarded act. Integrity is being single-minded in our devotion to God, leaving no room for pretense or hypocrisy.

Human dignity and self-esteem flow from high moral standards and personal integrity. We gain inner fulfillment as we strive to achieve worthwhile goals. Challenges and adversity are the crucible in which character is molded and tested. Stumbling blocks can be turned into stepping stones when we respond in the right way. Personal conduct rather than religious doctrine is the acid test of integrity. We should not merely listen to God's word and so deceive ourselves, but we should do what it says (James 1:22).

Experience may be the best teacher in our secular society but spiritual maturity is measured by wisdom and insight rather than the passing of the years. Great achievements involve taking risks and reaching beyond our grasp; climbing mountains of adversity gives the best view of opportunities. Achievements that involve little effort or risk are of little consequence. Lofty goals are inherent in a living faith; we cannot grow and remain the same. Growth inevitably means change, and spiritual growth means developing ever-deepening faith in God.

Just as there is an inherent law of supply and demand in the world of business, there is a spiritual law of *'Cause and Effect'* that regulates all human affairs. *Effect* follows *cause* just as surely as night follows day. Disregarding this spiritual law is the root cause of all self-inflicted adversity and much unhappiness. This spiritual law of 'Cause and Effect' is the way of love rather than self-centeredness, the way of giving rather than getting, the way of faith rather than doubt. The secular mind tends to blunt the sharp edge of the gospel truth. The carnal nature recognizes only the most obvious pleasures and transient rewards. It craves for an abundance of goods while the spiritual mind craves for an abundance of goodness.

Spiritual pride fails to recognize that whatever virtues we possess are through God's grace. When things are going our way, we have a tendency to forget God and trust in our own virtues. Even in the intellectual area of our lives, we often forget that our knowledge is largely the product of the labors of others. Pride can take many forms but it consists essentially of undue self-regard. It is the result of an inordinate sense of our own importance and is closely allied with vanity. A spirit of gratitude and humility tears away any mask of self-righteousness and makes us ever-conscious of our many blessings. The greatest lessons in gratitude and humility are learned from our good fortunes, while lessons in perseverance and character are learned from our trials and adversities. We cannot grow in the ways of God and remain the same.

Hypocrisy is pretending outwardly what we are not inwardly. To some degree, all of us suffer from this vice which is easily concealed in its mild form. However, when hypocrisy becomes ingrained and habitual in one's character, it takes on a mask of deception and self-righteousness. Much of life then becomes a charade which is self-destructive, undermining personal credibility and integrity. The central message of the Bible is sometimes clouded by the personality of its messenger. Even some Christian leaders find more meaning and comfort in being surrounded by power and authority then in living the simplicity of the gospel message. The spiritual concept of power and authority is a radical departure from what is understood by the secular world. The gospel message is not something separated from daily life but rather brings purpose and meaning into the life of every true believer.

Our conscience can become insensitive to wrongdoing when we habitually break God's moral and ethical laws. The human heart gravitates to those things which we value most. The conscience is an unwritten code of ethics which can become scarred and dulled until its whisper is no longer heard. Man-made laws can and do restrain bad behavior but they cannot alter character which is shaped by the inner voice of conscience. God's laws, unlike man-made laws, are timeless and perfect. We cannot purposely and habitually break these laws with impunity. The Ten Commandments are God's eternal guidelines for LIVINGWISE LIVINGWELL. The first four commandments define our relationship with God, while the remaining six commandments govern all human relationships.

A wholesome self-esteem is impossible when guilt has burrowed into the subconscious mind. Guilt is an unclean spiritual wound that festers with time. Guilt is to the soul what pain is to the body — a warning signal that something is amiss or wrong in our lives. The voice of conscience is a censor within the mind that is sensitive to wrongdoing. Prolonged feelings of guilt can undermine our health as there is no medical answer to misbehavior or wrongdoing.

The answer to feelings of guilt is to bring them out into the open where our conscious mind can analyze and identify their root cause. Then we should ask the Lord for forgiveness and resolve to be a better person in the future. The wonderful truth in the Christian life is God's unconditional love and forgiveness. The following is a suggested prayer:

> Almighty God, I confess my sinful nature in thought, word, and deed. I ask your forgiveness for all my sins of commission and omission. You alone, God, know how often I have sinned... in wandering from your ways, in wasting your gifts and in forgetting your love. Thank you for forgiving me, and help me to overcome my weaknesses. Amen.

Science and education can do little to alter our selfish sinful nature. All of us are infected by a human disease called sin which can only be cleansed by the Great Physician. Only the simple gospel message can change human hearts. God's promise of freedom from the bondage of sin is the central message of the gospel. The cardinal fact of human nature is that to some degree sin is in every one of us and those controlled by their sinful nature cannot please God. Sooner or later in our personal lives, our fallibility is thrust painfully and forcefully before our eyes. In such a moment of clarity, we fully realize the extent of our selfish, sinful nature. Time will reveal that the good within us comes only from knowing Christ as our personal friend and Savior.

For most individuals conversion is a process of change that happens over a period of time rather than in a blinding flash. It is an experience in which the conviction of sin in our lives causes us to recognize our need for a personal relationship with the God who created us. The process of conversion involves a deep sense of humility as we begin to realize that we do not really control our own destiny and that we need a Power greater than ourselves. During this period of profound change we begin to see that much of life is determined by invisible forces. This spiritual realm becomes just as real as the temporal realm in which we live.

Spiritual growth means change and having an ever-deepening faith and trust in God. Getting to know God and developing faith and trust is a gradual process as there are no shortcuts to spiritual growth. A man lived a life of crime, was finally caught, convicted and sent to prison. He had 20/20 vision but was spiritually blind. One Sunday he attended church service in the prison chapel during which a certain passage of Scripture left an unusual impact on him. The next day the Scripture verse was still on his mind; he asked for a Bible and began to search for the passage. Leafing through page after page without finding the verse, he decided that the only sure way of finding it was to begin reading Chapter 1 of Genesis and read every verse until he came to the one that he was looking for. The man read chapter after chapter, day after day, looking for the passage; the one that he wanted was in Hebrews which is near the end of the Bible. But long before he finally found it, he found Jesus Christ. This was the beginning of a new pilgrimage of faith, hope and love.

God created us to enjoy life through loving Him and loving one another. He is the source of all life and we should strive to harmonize the inner with the outer dimensions of our lives. This means that we should keep a balance between our *roots* and our *fruits*, between our faith and good works. While faith without good deeds is of little value, we cannot work our way to eternal life. Good works should be a natural by-product of our faith, not a substitute for it. Jesus was the supreme example for manifesting God's boundless love — the Word was made flesh that we may know the Way, the Truth and the Life.

Faith, hope and love remain; but the greatest of these is love (1 Cor. 13:13). Love is eternal and the very essence of our being. When we focus on the whole of life rather than its fragments we perceive everyone as needing love and wanting to extend love. Where there is no fear or anxiety, there is only love; and where there is only love, there we will find kindness and patience. Conditional love always has a price tag or strings attached but unconditional love is freely given and expects nothing in return.

Jesus' parable of the prodigal son (Luke 15:11-31) is a revealing lesson in unconditional love and forgiveness. The most moving description of love in the Bible is a penetrating summary of the character of Jesus found in Chapter 13 of 1 Corinthians. The central teaching of the New Testament proclaims that love is all powerful because God is Love. The life and teachings of Jesus as recorded in the four Gospels (Matthew, Mark, Luke, John) are the manifestations of God's boundless love.

Chapter 13 of 1 Corinthians capsules the most penetrating summary of love in the whole Bible. Love thrives on thoughtfulness but withers with neglect. The amazing power of love is unfathomable, miraculously increasing the more it is shared. Love cannot be stored or conserved for emergencies but craves for daily expression. The central teaching of the New Testament manifests the character of Jesus by proclaiming that love is at the heart of the universe (John 3:16) as well as the most important commandment (John 15:12). Jesus taught that we can fulfill our needs *only* as we help others fulfill their needs. This central principle became known as "The Law and the Prophets." It is a *Way of Life* that is diametrically opposite to the way of selfish human nature. It is the way of God-centered rather than self-centered living — the way of love rather than neglect, the way of giving rather than getting, the way of caring rather than indifference, the way of cooperation rather than competition.

In any growing relationship, the power of the attentive ear can be awesome. The art of good listening acknowledges the importance of the other individual by detecting feelings as well as hearing what is said. It involves feeling *with* the other individual, reading between the lines and detecting the real message that is spoken or sometimes unspoken. Most of us tend to be better talkers than listeners; real communication involves listening to the other person with total attention and patience.

Effective communication in a close relationship involves much more than merely hearing words spoken. Mutual empathy picks up little clues which may reveal a deep but unexpressed need. Empathy looks for and finds value and good in the other person even when it is not clearly evident. In a close relationship, each person feels free to expose inadequacies confident of acceptance in spite of imperfections.

Many individuals, particularly shut-ins, find Christian television programs entertaining and even spiritually helpful. They may offer drama, excitement, entertainment and even spiritual guidance, but it is the local pastor and congregation who are there when we need them. The TV evangelist may be a popular celebrity but he is not likely to visit us in our home or hospital. The local pastor, not the religious entertainer or celebrity, will be present for weddings, baptisms and funerals. Christian television programs can supplement but should never be a substitute for local church attendance. Loyalty and commitment should be first and foremost to the local church of our choice. The local church needs and deserves support through our prayers, our presence, our gifts and our service.

We can be raised in the church yet never be born in the Spirit. Church work is not necessarily the same as *the work of the church*. The church building is much more than a physical structure — it is the place *'from'* where we should go for service. Unfortunately in a large church, a stranger can remain a stranger after the service in a sea of faces that do not seem to care. The best service should begin when church worship ends. True Christianity should transcend religious denominations and not be bound by rituals and traditions. God is not honored by subservient obedience to religious laws and observances that are devoid of love. True religion comes from the heart; our lives are truly touched when we experience a personal encounter with God.

Tithing is an external expression of an internal commitment made in love. It is a spiritual adventure in faith that sets unseen forces in motion which bring untold blessings to the cheerful giver. Tithing should never be an act performed as a smokescreen to avoid surrendering important areas of our lives to God's will.

When we privately resolve to bring God from the fringe into the very center of our lives, things begin to happen. We begin altering some of our priorities, *making* time each day for quiet meditation and reflection. We daily give thanks for our many blessings which previously were taken for granted, recounting them one by one. As we quietly meditate on a few passages of Scripture, our mind focuses on some startling truths revealed to us for the first time. Before long we discover that God is no longer a stranger to us and that much of life is determined by invisible forces.

The spiritual realm can become just as real to us as the temporal one in which we live. It is an experience in which the conviction of sin in our lives causes us to recognize our need for a personal relationship with the God who created and loves us. We experience deep joy and inner peace from resolving to live in harmony with God's will, feeling and knowing that our thoughts and motives are right with God and right for us.

Meditation promotes spiritual health and general well-being. Through meditation we can undress our mind of the things of this world and delve to the very core of our being. By directing our thoughts toward God, the Creator and Author of all life, we develop greater perception and discernment of spiritual truths. Prayer should be a daily priority — seeking divine guidance through turning our thoughts to God. Setting aside even brief moments from a busy schedule to meditate can be remarkable in untangling the threads that often weave turmoil and confusion in our minds. Regular meditation enables our thoughts to gain a penetrating quality for discovering deeper truths about God and ourselves. Meditation brings us closer to God and increases our awareness of His presence.

Positive thoughts are more powerful than negative thoughts. When practiced habitually, positive thinking can gradually but surely dominate our outlook on life. Negative thoughts of doubt, insecurity, worry and anxiety diminish and ultimately wither from lack of nourishment. Irritations and frustrations are taken in stride when we realize that whatever is motivated by God's love is never a burden. External circumstances and events do not cause inner conficts or mental turmoil when we affirm and nourish our faith in God. The teachings of Jesus as contained in the four Gospels can be a daily source and resource for spiritual health. Deep joy and an enthusiasm for life come from living each day knowing that today well lived makes a happy memory of yesterday and a vision of hope for tomorrow. This is the day the Lord has made; let us rejoice and be glad in it! (Psalms 118:24).

Great hopes are lifegiving but 'feeble' expectations are lifedraining. Great hopes have an inspired vision of the future which trust in a *Power* greater than any problems. Many individuals go through life with an abstract nebulous faith that has little relevancy to their lives. Fear and doubt are enemies of faith but we gain inner strength in proportion to our faith and trust in God. He is sovereign and we can stake our lives on His sovereign promises. He rules and overrules every circumstance and event according to His ultimate plan.

The future is as bright as the promises of God — all things work together for good to those who love God. He is at work in all of us but we must have receptive hearts and be willing to do our part. A whole new dimension is added to our lives when our selfish nature is transformed by God's power and love. The foundation for lasting happiness lies in an ever-deepening faith and trust in God.

> On Christ the solid rock I stand
> All other ground is sinking sand

Fear knocked on my door; faith answered! Fear, worry and doubt shackle the mind and are enemies of faith. We are as young as our faith, as old as our doubts. The only positive thought that is stronger than fear is faith. Faith is being sure of what we hope for and certain of what we do not see. As our faith and trust in God grow stronger and deeper, we develop a personal philosophy of life that can sustain and encourage us in all situations. The noble simplicity of Christian faith and trust transcends all theological differences. The more that faith dominates our thinking, the less room is left for fear, worry and doubt. Strong dikes of faith will hold back any flood of fear. When we feed our faith, our doubts will starve to death. The real touchstone of Christian faith rests in the Scriptures.

Job was a righteous man who feared God and shunned evil. He was richly blessed with seven sons and three daughters, and became very wealthy with many sheep, camels, and oxen. Suddenly, his whole world began to crumble. All his family were killed, his livestock wiped out, he was besieged with boils from head to toe, and his relatives and friends forsook him. Being only human, Job could not understand why God allowed such terrible tragedies to occur. Job's faith and endurance were tested to the breaking point, yet he did not turn his back on God. Rather than succumbing to self-pity and allowing his spirit to become embittered, Job gained insight and wisdom through his suffering and adversity. Countless people, young and old alike, have surmounted appalling difficulties and overcome hopeless odds when they seemingly had reached a dead-end in their lives. Dormant power was suddenly activated through their unwavering faith in an all-powerful and loving God.

Belief has some degree of conviction based on intellect, but faith always embodies trust in the unseen. Happy individuals invariably have a spiritual dimension to their lives. They believe with conviction that God exists and created the universe. The greater their faith in God, the greater their inner peace and contentment. They know that God loves them even with all their shortcomings and weaknesses. Their faith brings a sense of order and purpose to their lives. They daily practice their faith through acts of kindness and love, trusting God in all things. Their faith is evident in their behavior which inevitably produces good works. Central to their Christian faith is the Incarnation — Jesus Christ, the Son of God, taking on human flesh.

An invisible spiritual law of *Cause and Effect* regulates all human affairs. It states that sooner or later a given set of circumstances or actions can be expected to produce certain consequences. The book of Proverbs conveys Solomon's divinely inspired observations of human nature whereby general truths are brought to bear on specific situations. The Old Testament tells us what not to do (the difference between right and wrong), while the New Testament tells us what to do (love one another as Christ loves us). The key to greater understanding of God's Word is to put it into practice in our daily lives. This demands personal commitment which affects our priorities and basic values in life. Situations inevitably arise that will test and strengthen our faith and have a profound effect on our character.

The test of our understanding of God's Word is simply by how we live day-in and day-out. An excellent program for spiritual growth and inspiration involves setting aside a quiet time to read the four gospels in the New Testament (Matthew, Mark, Luke, John). The same passages can be read again and again, each time with fresh meaning and greater understanding. Concentrated, repetitive reading enables us to better grasp the full meaning and depth of Scriptural truths. Memorizing those passages that relate to our deepest needs also has a therapeutic and healing effect on the mind and the body. Following this time in solitude, we should ask ourselves: "What is God saying to me, and how can I apply His teaching today?"

The Bible is a treasure house of wisdom and inspiration, and is God's manual for LIVINGWISE LIVINGWELL. The best way to prove the relevancy of the Bible in one's personal life is to put it to the test by doing what it says. It is more than just a book of ethical guides for right living; it is a *love letter* from God to all of us. He speaks to us through the Bible which is the *only* authoritative basis for how to live and what to believe. It was written by men who were chosen by God and inspired by the Holy Spirit. In our confused and spiritually bankrupt world, the Bible speaks to us as no other book. Priceless treasures of wisdom and knowledge are hidden in God's Word. The universal truths revealed through the Scriptures are as relevant today as two thousand years ago simply because God does not change and human nature does not change.

God's character is vividly revealed in the life of His Son, Jesus Christ. The secret of Jesus' power over the hearts and minds of people in all walks of life is revealed in His teaching. He was a friend to the friendless and He spoke with unquestioned authority for He was truly the Son of the living God. He gave us illuminating contradictions that confound human logic — the first shall be last, the weakest the strongest, the poorest the richest, the simple the profound, the mortal the immortal. These and many other captivating and meaningful truths are revealed in His teachings.

The greatest sermon ever given was 'The Sermon on the Mount' (Matthew 5,6,7) spoken by Jesus Christ two thousand years ago. It begins with eight Beatitudes (Matthew 5:3-10) which are deeply profound yet amazingly simple. These Beatitudes are nothing less than God's own character put into words. These eternal and unchanging truths for personal happiness are as modern as tomorrow. Love is at the heart of the Beatitudes. The more we apply the spirit of the Beatitudes in all areas of our daily lives, the easier it becomes to rise above injustices and adversities. As we bring Christ from the periphery to the center of our lives, we gain more and more inner strength, wisdom and insight.

"Happy are the poor in spirit for theirs is the kingdom of heaven." This Beatitude conveys genuine humility that comes from knowing how much we need God in our daily lives. We trust in God's love and power at all times, and strive to develop Christlike attitudes by having a close personal relationship with God. The greatest obstacle to a spirit of genuine humility is having an inordinate sense of our own importance and accomplishments.

"Happy are they that mourn, for they will be comforted." This Beatitude requires a compassionate heart that is sensitive to the feelings and needs of others. In a spiritual sense we are to care deep down inside about our relationship with God. As a result we experience a meaningful prayer-life, with our prime purpose in life being to serve God by meeting the needs of others.

"Happy are the meek, for they will inherit the earth." This Beatitude calls us to be patient, gentle and kind, yielding all our rights to God. The real test of meekness is having self-control. The reward is victory over anger, bitterness and resentment.

"Happy are those who hunger and thirst for righteousness, for they will be filled." This Beatitude involves earnestly seeking to know God better through a systematic plan for studying God's Word. The ultimate goal should be to make every principle and truth of Scripture a reality in our daily lives. The rewards of continual spiritual growth are greater joy, fulfillment and understanding of God's Word.

"Happy are the merciful, for they will be shown mercy." This Beatitude petitions us to be sympathetic and understanding, forgiving those who may offend us. By doing so, we are communicating God's love to others.

"Happy are the pure in heart, for they will see God." This Beatitude signifies a willingness to allow the Holy Spirit to control every area of our lives, cleansing us of all impure thoughts and motives.

"Happy are the peacemakers, for they will be called sons of God." This Beatitude requires us to go out of our way to make things right with others, admitting our shortcomings and wrongdoings. Criticism begets criticism, but praise begets praise. We must accept responsibility for our thoughts, words and deeds. The spirit of this Beatitude projects genuine Christian love.

"*Happy* are those who are persecuted because of righteousness, for theirs is the kingdom of heaven." This Beatitude requires a deep faith and trust in God, and being willing to stand out from the crowd rather than being lost in it. This Beatitude requires boldness in witnessing our faith and refusal to compromise our principles or values.

The author of this book *LIVINGWISE LIVINGWELL* recommends the New International Version of the Bible. Italicized sectional headings are inserted throughout which are highly beneficial to the reader. Clarity and ease of reading are dominant features of this NIV accurate translation. The NIV Bible cuts through outdated words and obscure meanings of older versions, allowing the reader to harvest scriptural truths more easily. Recommended by over twenty denominations, it is the ideal Bible for anyone new to God's Word, young and old alike. More than sixty-five million copies of the NIV edition have been distributed around the world.

The New International Version (NIV) of the Holy Bible was published in 1978. The translation by over a hundred distinguished scholars had its beginning in 1965 using the best available Hebrew, Aramaic and Greek texts. Participants from the United States, Great Britain, Canada, Australia and New Zealand working together gave the project its international scope. To safeguard the translation from sectarian bias, the distinguished scholars were from many denominations including Anglican, Assemblies of God, Baptist, Brethren, Christian Reformed, Church of Christ, Evangelical, Lutheran, Mennonite, Methodist, Nazarene, Presbyterian and Wesleyan. Each one of the sixty-six books of the Bible underwent three successive revisions and examinations for faithfulness to the original. The NIV Bible translation committee's goals were accuracy, clarity and literary quality. The translators were united in their commitment to the authority and infallibility of the Bible as God's Word, which contains the divine answer to the deepest needs of humanity.

WHERE TO FIND
Love Defined (1 Corinthians 13:1-13)
The Greatest Commandment (Matthew 22:34-40)
The Beatitudes (Matthew 5:3-12)
The Lord's Prayer (Matthew 6:5-15)
The Shepard Psalm (Psalms 23)

THE LIFE OF JESUS
His Birth (Matthew 1:18-25 & 2:1-15, Luke 1:26-56 & 2:1-40)
His Youth (Luke 2:41-52)

His Baptism (Matthew 3:all, Mark 1:1-11)
His Temptation (Matthew 4:1-11, Luke 4:1-13)
His Sermon on the Mount (Matthew 5,6,7:all, Luke 6:17-49)
His Triumphal Entry into Jerusalem (Matthew 21:1-11, Mark 11:1-11, Luke 19:29-55, John 12:12-19)
The Easter Story (Matthew 26-28 incl:all, Mark 14-16 incl:all, Luke 22-24 incl:all, John 13-21 inclusive:all)

THE PARABLES OF JESUS
The Sower (Matthew 13:1-23)
The Weeds (Matthew 13:24-30 & 36-43)
The Net (Matthew 13:47-52)
The Lost Sheep (Matthew 18:12-14)
The Unmerciful Servant (Matthew 18:21-35)
The Laborers in the Vineyard (Matthew 20:1-16)
The Vineyard (Matthew 21:33-46)
The Ten Virgins (Matthew 25:1-13)
The Talents (Matthew 25:14-30)
The Sheep and the Goats (Matthew 25:31-46)
The Good Samaritan (Luke 10:25-37)
The Rich Fool (Luke 12:16-21)
The Barren Fig Tree (Luke 13:6-9)
The Lost Sheep (Luke 15:3-7)
The Prodigal Son (Luke 15:11-32)
The Rich Ruler (Luke 18:18-29)
The Vine and the Branches (John 15:1-17)

OUR PERSONAL LIFE
Discouragment (Psalms 23,42,43)
Frustration (Psalms 40,73,90; Hebrews 12)
Worry (Psalms 46; Matthew 6:25-34)
Tension (Psalms 91; James 5:7-11)
Weariness (Isaiah 40:28-31; Matthew 11:28-30)
Boredom (2 Kings 5; Job 38; Psalms 103 & 104; Ephesians 3)
Tranquility (Ecclesiastes 3:1-15)
Insomnia (Psalms 4,56,130)
Loneliness (Psalms 27 & 91; Luke 8; 1 Peter 4)
Rejection (Colossians 1; 1 Peter 1; Romans 8)
Jealousy (Psalms 49; James 3)
Temptation (Psalms 15,19,139; Matthew 4; James 4)
Forgiveness (Psalms 51; Matthew 23; Luke 15)
Faith (Hebrews 11)

Sickness (Psalms 6,39,41,67; Isaiah 26)
Bereavement (1 Corinthians 15; 1 Thessalonians 4:13-18)
Resentment (Luke 6; 2 Corinthians 4; Ephesians 4)
Marriage (Proverbs 5:15-21, Proverbs 31:10-31)
Wisdom (Proverbs 1-9 incl.)
Proverbs (Proverbs 10-29 incl.)

In our pilgrimage through life, spiritual growth occurs whenever we take a *voluntary* step towards allowing God to improve the quality of our lives. These voluntary steps can take many forms, but there is no better way of getting to know about the character of God than by reading and meditating on passages of Scripture. The finite human mind can never fully grasp the boundless love and power of God. The Holy Bible is able to make us wise, for all Scripture is the Word of God which thoroughly equips us for good works. The greatest deeds are those done in a Christlike attitude which comes from spiritual wisdom. The wisdom that comes from God is first of all pure; then peace-loving, considerate, submissive, full of mercy and good fruit, impartial and sincere. The greatest book ever written reveals an all-powerful but personal and loving God. In the New Testament of the Bible we find that the WORD was made flesh, revealing the Way, the Truth and the Life for all of us.

Affirmation of Christian Faith
I believe in God the Father, infinite in wisdom, power and love. I believe in Jesus Christ, God's only Son and gift of His unfailing grace. I believe in the Holy Spirit which is the divine presence in my life whereby I find strength and help in time of need. I believe that this faith should manifest itself daily in my life.